AF726530

1995 Supplement

to

Cases and Materials

on

CRIMINAL JUSTICE ADMINISTRATION

By

FRANK W. MILLER
James Carr Professor Emeritus of Criminal Jurisprudence,
Washington University

ROBERT O. DAWSON
Bryant Smith Chair in Law,
University of Texas

GEORGE E. DIX
A.W. Walker Centennial Chair in Law,
University of Texas

RAYMOND I. PARNAS
Professor of Law, University of California, Davis

FOURTH EDITION

Westbury, New York
THE FOUNDATION PRESS, INC.
1995

COPYRIGHT © 1991–1994 THE FOUNDATION PRESS, INC.

COPYRIGHT © 1995

By

THE FOUNDATION PRESS, INC.
All rights reserved

ISBN 1–56662–301–4

TEXT IS PRINTED ON 10% POST CONSUMER RECYCLED PAPER

PRINTED WITH SOY INK™

PREFACE

Continuing developments, most significantly decisions of the Supreme Court of the United States, continue to make supplementation of the materials necessary. This supplement contains primarily decisions of the Supreme Court. Relevant cases decided before the summer recess of the Court's October, 1994 Term are included.

Many of the footnotes from reprinted decisions have been omitted. Where this has been done, those footnotes retained have not been renumbered. Deletions of footnotes and textual citations to authority have been made without specific indication of these omissions.

F.W.M.
R.O.D.
G.E.D.
R.I.P.

July 10, 1995

*

TABLE OF CONTENTS

CHAPTER 4 DETENTIONS OF PERSONS AND RELATED SEARCHES

B. Field Detentions and Related Searches

B. The Grand Jury

CHAPTER 15. RIGHT TO A SPEEDY TRIAL

A. Sixth Amendment Speedy Trial Guarantee

CHAPTER 16. COMPETENCY TO STAND TRIAL

A. The Duty to Inquire Into Competency

B. Processing of Incompetent Defendants

CHAPTER 17. DISCOVERY AND DISCLOSURE

A. Prosecutorial Disclosure

1. Constitutional Obligations

B. Disclosure by the Defense

CHAPTER 18. RIGHT TO AN IMPARTIAL TRIAL

CHAPTER 19. JOINDER AND SEVERANCE OF CHARGES AND DEFENDANTS

B. Joinder and Severance of Defendants

CHAPTER 20. DOUBLE JEOPARDY

A. Former Acquittal

B. Multiple Convictions

C. Termination Without Acquittal or Conviction

1. Mistrials

CHAPTER 22. ADJUDICATION OF GUILT BY PLEA

A. Entry of the Plea of Guilty

C. Plea Bargaining

4. The Necessity of Respecting a Bargain Once Made

CHAPTER 23. ADJUDICATION OF GUILT OR INNOCENCE BY TRIAL

A. Proof Beyond a Reasonable Doubt

B. Right to Trial by Jury

1. Prosecutions to Which the Right Applies

2. Composition of the Jury

3. The Jury Size and Agreement Required

C. Confrontation, Cross-Examination and Compulsory Process to Obtain Witnesses

1. Confrontation

CHAPTER 24. EFFECTIVE ASSISTANCE OF COUNSEL

A. Right to Have Counsel Be "Effective"

CHAPTER 25. SENTENCING

B. Structuring the Sentencing System

2. Controlling Sentencing Discretion by Appellate Review

a. Appellate Review of Sentencing Considerations

b. Appellate Review of Sentences Imposed

3. Reducing Discretion by "Determinate" Sentencing

b. Federal Reform: The Sentencing Reform Act of 1984

CHAPTER 26. APPEAL AND COLLATERAL ATTACK

B. Appeal

C. Collateral Attack

TABLE OF CASES

Principal cases are in italic type. Non-principal cases are in roman type. References are to Pages.

1995 Supplement

to

Cases and Materials

on

CRIMINAL JUSTICE ADMINISTRATION

*

Part One

INVESTIGATION OF CRIME

Chapter 1

THE EXCLUSIONARY SANCTION

A. ADOPTION OF THE FEDERAL CONSTITUTIONAL EXCLUSIONARY SANCTION

Page 28. Add the following to the notes after Mapp v. Ohio:

6. The effectiveness of the Fourth Amendment exclusionary rule was explored in Heffernan and Lovely, Evaluating the Fourth Amendment Exclusionary Rule: The Problem of Police Compliance with the Law, 24 U.Mich.J.L.Reform 311 (1991). After noting the difficulty of empirical study in this area, the authors discussed their own efforts, which involved the administration of questionnaires to 547 police officers in four midsized police departments. The questionnaires were designed to determine officers' awareness of what Fourth Amendment law requires in six areas (based upon Supreme Court decisions) and the officers' willingness to avoid violating those requirements. Three of the scenarios presented involved situations that the Supreme Court has held do not permit police intervention; this was recognized by 57%, 54%, and 78% of the officers respectively. Id. at 332. Those officers with advanced in-service training were more likely than other officers to recognize what the law required. Id. at 338. The authors noted:

> [E]ven the most knowledgeable officers * * * make a substantial number of mistakes in dealing with the rules of search and seizure. * * * *[T]he findings indicate that, even if all police officers were disposed to adhere to the rules of search and seizure, there would nonetheless be substantial deviation from those rules as they are presently constituted because of police mistakes about what they require.*

Id. at 338–39 (emphasis in original). Turning to whether officers are in fact disposed to adhere to the rules of search and seizure, the authors found that in the three scenarios presenting situations in which no police intervention was legally authorized, 24%, 19% and 4% of the officers who recognized that the law barred police action nevertheless indicated they would take action. Id. at 346. The first scenario, which elicited the most dramatic knowing noncompliance, was based upon Ybarra v. Illinois, 444 U.S. 85, 100 S.Ct. 338, 62 L.Ed.2d 238 (1979) (discussed in the text on pages 176–178), holding that officers executing a search warrant could not search all persons found on the premises. Officers' commitment to complying with what they understand to be the law's requirements did not increase with greater in-service training. Id. at 354. Since the authors avoided directly asking officers whether they would take action they believed was illegal, the questionnaire did not address the officers' rationale for taking action. Id. at 351.

B. "STANDING," FRUIT OF THE POISONOUS TREE AND ATTENUATION OF THE TAINT

Page 39. Add the following to note 5 after Wong Sun v. United States:

One possible qualification to the general rule that the manner in which the defendant is brought before the court will not affect the court's jurisdiction was at issue in United States v. Alvarez–Machain, 504 U.S. 655, 112 S.Ct. 2188, 119 L.Ed.2d 441 (1992). The Ninth Circuit Court of Appeals had held that a defendant in a federal criminal prosecution could challenge the jurisdiction of the court over him on the basis that he was brought into the United States from a foreign country in violation of a treaty between the United States and that foreign country, *if* the foreign country had itself protested the effort by the federal court to exercise jurisdiction over the defendant. Such a defendant would be derivatively asserting the right of the foreign country under the treaty. The Supreme Court did not reach whether this was a correct construction of the law, because it found that the treaty invoked by the defendant—the Extradition Treaty between the United States and Mexico—did not bar the defendant's abduction in Mexico and transportation to the United States by persons acting at the instigation of United States law enforcement officers. The Treaty, as construed by the Court, obligates under certain circumstances the United States and Mexico to extradite individuals to the other country and provides procedures to be used when this is done. But it does not prohibit either country from ignoring the extradition procedure and simply abducting an individual from the other country. An abduction of the sort in the case, the majority acknowledged, might violate "general international law principles." But the treaty did not incorporate those principles into its terms. Since the abduction of Alvarez–Machain from Mexico did not violate Mexico's rights under the treaty, there was no such violation for Alvarez–Machain to derivatively assert as a basis for challenging the federal courts' exercise of jurisdiction over him. The rule of *Ker* was consequently "fully applicable," and "[Alvarez–Machain's] forcible abduction does not therefore prohibit his trial in a court of the United States for violations of the criminal law of the United States." 504 U.S. at 670, 112 S.Ct. at 2197, 119 L.Ed.2d at 456.

C. GOOD FAITH AND OTHER EXCEPTIONS

Page 58: Add the following new note after United States v. Leon:

1a. Does the *Leon* good faith exception apply if no valid warrant actually exists but an officer reasonably believes it does? The issue was presented in Arizona v. Evans, ___ U.S. ___, 115 S.Ct. 1185, 131 L.Ed.2d 34 (1995), in which Evans had been stopped by a Phoenix police officer for a traffic offense. The officer entered Evans' name into a computer terminal located in the patrol car and he received a message in reply indicating that there was an outstanding misdemeanor warrant for Evans' arrest. Based on his belief that such a warrant existed, the officer placed Evans under arrest and in the process discovered marijuana. In fact, an arrest warrant had been issued for Evans but it had been quashed 17 days before his arrest. When Evans was prosecuted for possession of the marijuana, he sought suppression of the substance. Testimony at the hearing on his motion established that the warrant had been for nonappearance on traffic tickets and when Evans appeared before a Justice of the Peace, the justice made a notation on the file to "quash warrant." Evidence also showed that standard procedure in such a case was for a justice court clerk to telephone the sheriff's office and inform that office that the warrant had been quashed. The sheriff's office would then remove the warrant from its computer records. Evans' file did not contain the notion usually made when the clerk called the sheriff's office and the sheriff's office had no record of a call from the clerk. Without making any findings regarding whether the error had been made by the court clerk or the sheriff, the trial court suppressed the marijuana. The Arizona Supreme Court upheld this action, indicating that it attached no significance to whether the error was made by a court employee or law enforcement personnel.

The Supreme Court reversed. The Arizona Supreme Court's conclusion that suppression was required even if responsibility for the error rested with the clerk of the justice court "is contrary to the reasoning of [*Leon, Sheppard,* and *Krull*]." Chief Justice Rehnquist continued for the Court:

> If court employees were responsible for the erroneous computer record, the exclusion of evidence at trial would not sufficiently deter future errors so as to warrant such a severe sanction. First, as we noted in *Leon,* the exclusionary rule was historically designed as a means of deterring police misconduct, not mistakes by court employees. Second, respondent offers no evidence that court employees are inclined to ignore or subvert the Fourth Amendment or that lawlessness among these actors requires application of the extreme sanction of exclusion. To the contrary, the Chief Clerk of the Justice Court testified at the suppression hearing that this type of error occurred once every three or four years.
>
> Finally, and most important, there is no basis for believing that application of the exclusionary rule in these circumstances will have a significant effect on court employees responsible for informing the police that a warrant has been quashed. Because court clerks are not adjuncts to the law enforcement team engaged in the often competitive enterprise of ferreting out crime, they have no stake in the outcome of particular criminal prosecutions. The threat of exclusion of evidence could not be expected to deter such individuals from failing to inform police officials that a warrant had been quashed.
>
> If it were indeed a court clerk who was responsible for the erroneous entry on the police computer, application of the exclusionary rule also could not be expected to alter the behavior of the arresting officer. As the trial court in this case stated: "I think the police officer [was] bound to arrest. I think he would [have been] derelict in his duty if he failed to arrest." The Chief Clerk of the Justice Court testified that this type of error occurred "on[c]e every three or four years." In fact, once the court clerks discovered the error, they immediately corrected it, and then proceeded to search their files to make sure that no similar mistakes had occurred. There is no indication that the arresting officer was not acting objectively reasonable when he relied upon the police computer record. Application of the *Leon* framework supports a categorical exception to the exclusionary rule for clerical errors of court employees.

___ U.S. at ___, 115 S.Ct. at 1193–94, 131 L.Ed.2d at 46–47. The Court explicitly refused to address whether a similar analysis would be applied to determine whether the evidence would have to be suppressed if "police personnel" were responsible for the error. ___ U.S. at ___ n. 5, 115 S.Ct. at 1194 n. 5, 131 L.Ed.2d at 46 n. 5. It remanded the case to the Arizona Supreme Court for further proceedings not inconsistent with the Supreme Court's opinion.

Justice Stevens dissented on the merits of the basic issue:

> *Leon* stands for the dubious but limited proposition that courts should not look behind the face of a warrant on which police have relied in good faith. The *Leon* Court's exemption of judges and magistrates from the deterrent ambit of the exclusionary rule rested, consistently with the emphasis on the warrant requirement, on those officials' constitutionally determined role in issuing warrants. Taken on its own terms, *Leon's* logic does not extend to the time after the warrant has issued; nor does it extend to court clerks and functionaries, some of whom work in the same building with police officers and may have more regular and direct contact with police than with judges or magistrates.

___ U.S. at ___, 115 S.Ct. at 1196, 131 L.Ed.2d at 50–51 (Stevens, J., dissenting). Justice Ginsburg, joined by Justice Stevens, dissented on the ground that the Arizona court's ruling should be regarded as based on state rather than federal constitutional law. Justice O'Connor, joined by Justices Souter and Breyer, joined the opinion of the Court but wrote separately to comment:

> In limiting itself to [the] single question [whether a court employee's departure from established procedure is the kind of error to which the exclusionary rule should apply], * * * the Court does not hold that the court employee's mistake in this case was necessarily the only error that may have occurred and to which the exclusionary rule might apply. While the police were innocent of the court employee's mistake, they may or may not have acted reasonably in their reliance on the recordkeeping system itself. Surely it would not be reasonable for the police to rely, say, on a recordkeeping system, their own or some other agency's, that has no mechanism to ensure its accuracy over time and that routinely leads to false arrests, even years after the probable cause for any such arrest has ceased to exist (if it ever existed).
>
> * * *
>
> In recent years, we have witnessed the advent of powerful, computer-based recordkeeping systems that facilitate arrests in ways that have never before been possible. The police, of course, are entitled to enjoy the substantial advantages this technology confers. They may not, however, rely on it blindly. With the benefits of more efficient law enforcement mechanisms comes the burden of corresponding constitutional responsibilities.

___ U.S. at ___, 115 S.Ct. at 1194–95, 131 L.Ed.2d at 48 (O'Connor, J., concurring).

Chapter 2

CONSTITUTIONAL DOCTRINES RELATING TO LAW ENFORCEMENT CONDUCT

B. THE FOURTH AMENDMENT'S PROHIBITION AGAINST UNREASONABLE SEARCHES AND SEIZURES

2. POLICE ACTIVITY CONSTITUTING A "SEIZURE"

Page 105. Insert the following in the introductory text after the paragraph beginning, "*Definition of 'Seizures.'*"

The Supreme Court again addressed the Fourth Amendment's coverage of "seizures" in Soldal v. Cook County, Illinois, ___ U.S. ___, 113 S.Ct. 538, 121 L.Ed.2d 450 (1992), a civil case. Soldal's trailer home had been removed from its location in a mobile home park by the park owners, acting illegally under state law but with the active protection of local police. He sued for civil damages under 42 U.S.C.A. § 1983, claiming a conspiracy to unreasonably seize and remove his trailer. The district court granted summary judgment for the defendants; the Court of Appeals affirmed, reasoning that the defendants had not "seized" Soldal's trailer within the meaning of the Fourth Amendment.

A unanimous Supreme Court reversed. The Court of Appeals, Justice White explained, had construed the Fourth Amendment as not covering "technical" seizures that infringe neither privacy nor liberty interests. No seizure therefore occurred since the officers had not invaded Soldal's privacy by entering or rummaging through the house or his liberty by detaining him. *Katz* and its progeny make clear, Justice White responded for the Court, that property rights "are not the sole measure of Fourth Amendment violations." That case law did not, however, signal abandonment of the previously recognized protection for property under the Amendment. "[O]ur cases unmistakably hold," he emphasized, "that the [Fourth] Amendment protects property as well as privacy." ___ U.S. at ___, 113 S.Ct. at 544, 121 L.Ed.2d at 459.

The Court of Appeals had reasoned that the "plain view" seizure cases—such as Horton v. California, 496 U.S. 128, 110 S.Ct. 2301, 110 L.Ed.2d 112 (1990), reprinted on page 106 of the text—reflect that the Fourth Amendment protects against seizures that are the result of a "search," but do not reflect coverage of "seizures" generally. This reading of the "plain view" cases was faulty, Justice White explained:

> [A]n officer who happens to come across an individual's property in a public area could seize it only if Fourth Amendment standards are

> satisfied—for example, if the items are evidence of a crime or contraband.

___ U.S. at ___, 113 S.Ct. at 547, 121 L.Ed.2d at 463.

Soldal's complaint, the Court concluded, alleged not simply a " 'garden-variety' landlord-tenant or commercial dispute" below Fourth Amendment recognition. Rather, it alleged a situation that plainly implicated the interests protected by the Fourth Amendment and thus constituted a "seizure" within the meaning of that provision. ___ U.S. at ___, 113 S.Ct. at 549, 121 L.Ed.2d at 465.

4. APPLYING THE "STANDING" REQUIREMENT IN SEARCH AND SEIZURE

Page 124. Add the following new note after Rakas v. Illinois:

3. The Supreme Court reaffirmed both the standing requirement and its *Rakas* application in United States v. Padilla, ___ U.S. ___, 113 S.Ct. 1936, 123 L.Ed.2d 635 (1993) (per curiam), involving the stop of an automobile owned by Donald and Maria Simpson but driven by Luis Arciniega. Arciniega consented to a search of the car and the officers discovered 560 pounds of cocaine in the trunk. Arciniega agreed to cooperate with law enforcement officials. Pursuant to the conspiracy of which he was a part, Arciniega telephoned Jorge and Maria Padilla. They met Arciniega and were arrested as they attempted to drive away in the car. Further investigation implicated Xavier Padilla, who was married to Maria Padilla. The Simpsons and all three Padillas were prosecuted for conspiracy to possess and distribute the cocaine and with possession of it. They challenged the stop of the vehicle and the resulting discovery of the drug. Under the case law of the United States Court of Appeals for the Ninth Circuit, the standing requirement was subject to a "coconspirator exception," which permitted challenges to searches by a co-conspirator who lacked ordinary standing but was shown to have had either a supervisory role in the conspiracy or joint control over the place or property involved in the search or seizure. Under this doctrine, the Ninth Circuit held that both Simpsons and Xavier Padilla could challenge the stop of the vehicle; it remanded for the district court to determine whether Jorge and Maria Padilla shared sufficient responsibility for the enterprise to give them standing under its rule. The Supreme Court held that the Ninth Circuit exception was contrary to the Court's prior holdings and at odds with the principles reflected in cases such as *Rakas,* and therefore the Ninth Circuit erred in applying it.

> Expectations of privacy and property interests govern the analysis of Fourth Amendment search and seizure claims. Participants in a criminal conspiracy may have such expectations or interests, but the conspiracy itself neither adds nor detracts from them.

___ U.S. at ___, 113 S.Ct. at 1939, 123 L.Ed.2d at 641. The court remanded the case to the Ninth Circuit for that court to consider whether each defendant "had either a property interest protected by the Fourth Amendment that was interfered with by the stop of the automobile driven by Arciniega, or a reasonable expectation of privacy that was invaded by the search thereof."

Chapter 3

ISSUANCE AND EXECUTION OF ARREST AND SEARCH WARRANTS

C. THE REQUIREMENT OF PARTICULARITY AND EXECUTION OF WARRANTS

Page 179. Add the following to note 6 after Maryland v. Garrison:

The Supreme Court addressed the Fourth Amendment issue in Wilson v. Arkansas, ___ U.S. ___, 115 S.Ct. 1914, 131 L.Ed.2d 976 (1995). Holding that the Arkansas court erred in concluding that the Fourth Amendment imposed no "knock and announce" requirement, the Supreme Court reviewed the common law authority requiring announcement and continued:

> Our own cases have acknowledged that the common-law principle of announcement is "embedded in Anglo–American law," but we have never squarely held that this principle is an element of the reasonableness inquiry under the Fourth Amendment. We now so hold. Given the longstanding common-law endorsement of the practice of announcement, we have little doubt that the Framers of the Fourth Amendment thought that the method of an officer's entry into a dwelling was among the factors to be considered in assessing the reasonableness of a search or seizure. Contrary to the decision below, we hold that in some circumstances an officer's unannounced entry into a home might be unreasonable under the Fourth Amendment.
>
> This is not to say, of course, that every entry must be preceded by an announcement. The Fourth Amendment's flexible requirement of reasonableness should not be read to mandate a rigid rule of announcement that ignores countervailing law enforcement interests. As even petitioner concedes, the common-law principle of announcement was never stated as an inflexible rule requiring announcement under all circumstances.
>
> Indeed, at the time of the framing, the common-law admonition that an officer "ought to signify the cause of his coming," had not been extended conclusively to the context of felony arrests. The common-law principle gradually was applied to cases involving felonies, but at the same time the courts continued to recognize that under certain circumstances the presumption in favor of announcement necessarily would give way to contrary considerations.
>
> Thus, because the common-law rule was justified in part by the belief that announcement generally would avoid "the destruction or breaking of any house ... by which great damage and inconvenience might ensue," courts acknowledged that the presumption in favor of announcement would yield under circumstances presenting a threat of physical violence. See, e.g., Read v. Case, 4 Conn. 166, 170 (1822) (plaintiff who "had resolved ... to resist even to the shedding of blood ... was not within the reason and spirit of the rule requiring notice"); Mahomed v. The Queen, 4 Moore 239, 247, 13

Eng.Rep. 293, 296 (P.C.1843) ("While he was firing pistols at them, were they to knock at the door, and to ask him to be pleased to open it for them? The law in its wisdom only requires this ceremony to be observed when it possibly may be attended with some advantage, and may render the breaking open of the outer door unnecessary"). Similarly, courts held that an officer may dispense with announcement in cases where a prisoner escapes from him and retreats to his dwelling. See, e.g., ibid.; Allen v. Martin, 10 Wend. 300, 304 (N.Y.Sup.Ct.1833). Proof of "demand and refusal" was deemed unnecessary in such cases because it would be a "senseless ceremony" to require an officer in pursuit of a recently escaped arrestee to make an announcement prior to breaking the door to retake him. Id., at 304. Finally, courts have indicated that unannounced entry may be justified where police officers have reason to believe that evidence would likely be destroyed if advance notice were given.

We need not attempt a comprehensive catalog of the relevant countervailing factors here. For now, we leave to the lower courts the task of determining the circumstances under which an unannounced entry is reasonable under the Fourth Amendment. We simply hold that although a search or seizure of a dwelling might be constitutionally defective if police officers enter without prior announcement, law enforcement interests may also establish the reasonableness of an unannounced entry.

___ U.S. at ___, 115 S.Ct. at 1918–19, 131 L.Ed.2d at ___. The Court summarized the facts of the case before it:

During November and December 1992, petitioner Sharlene Wilson made a series of narcotics sales to an informant acting at the direction of the Arkansas State Police. In late November, the informant purchased marijuana and methamphetamine at the home that petitioner shared with Bryson Jacobs. On December 30, the informant telephoned petitioner at her home and arranged to meet her at a local store to buy some marijuana. According to testimony presented below, petitioner produced a semiautomatic pistol at this meeting and waved it in the informant's face, threatening to kill her if she turned out to be working for the police. Petitioner then sold the informant a bag of marijuana.

The next day, police officers applied for and obtained warrants to search petitioner's home and to arrest both petitioner and Jacobs. Affidavits filed in support of the warrants set forth the details of the narcotics transactions and stated that Jacobs had previously been convicted of arson and firebombing. The search was conducted later that afternoon. Police officers found the main door to petitioner's home open. While opening an unlocked screen door and entering the residence, they identified themselves as police officers and stated that they had a warrant. Once inside the home, the officers seized marijuana, methamphetamine, valium, narcotics paraphernalia, a gun, and ammunition. They also found petitioner in the bathroom, flushing marijuana down the toilet.

___ U.S. at ___, 115 S.Ct. at 1915–16, 131 L.Ed.2d at ___. Regarding the application of its newly-announced law to these facts, the Court reasoned:

Respondent contends that the judgment below should be affirmed because the unannounced entry in this case was justified for two reasons. First, respondent argues that police officers reasonably believed that a prior

> announcement would have placed them in peril, given their knowledge that petitioner had threatened a government informant with a semiautomatic weapon and that Mr. Jacobs had previously been convicted of arson and firebombing. Second, respondent suggests that prior announcement would have produced an unreasonable risk that petitioner would destroy easily disposable narcotics evidence.
>
> These considerations may well provide the necessary justification for the unannounced entry in this case. Because the Arkansas Supreme Court did not address their sufficiency, however, we remand to allow the state courts to make any necessary findings of fact and to make the determination of reasonableness in the first instance.

___ U.S. at ___, 115 S.Ct. at 1919, 131 L.Ed.2d at ___. The state court's judgment was therefore reversed and the case remanded for further proceedings not inconsistent with the Supreme Court's opinion.

But if entry to execute a warrant violates the Fourth Amendment requirements developed in *Wilson,* what are the consequences? In *Wilson,* the Court added:

> Respondent and its amici also ask us to affirm the denial of petitioner's suppression motion on an alternative ground: that exclusion is not a constitutionally compelled remedy where the unreasonableness of a search stems from the failure of announcement. Analogizing to the "independent source" doctrine * * *, and the "inevitable discovery" rule * * *, respondent and its amici argue that any evidence seized after an unreasonable, unannounced entry is causally disconnected from the constitutional violation and that exclusion goes beyond the goal of precluding any benefit to the government flowing from the constitutional violation. Because this remedial issue was not addressed by the court below and is not within the narrow question on which we granted certiorari, we decline to address these arguments.

___ U.S. at ___ n. 3, 115 S.Ct. at 1918 n. 3, 131 L.Ed.2d at ___ n. 3.

Page 180. Add the following at the end of note 6 after Maryland v. Garrison:

In 1994, the Wisconsin Supreme Court reconsidered *Cleveland* and overruled it:

> *Cleveland* required that in order to justify a no-knock entry, the police must be able to set forth the exigent circumstances with sufficient particularity to show reasonable cause to believe that the exigent circumstances exist. To justify no-knock entry to prevent the destruction of evidence under *Cleveland,* the police cannot rely on a "blanket" rule that no-knock entry is justified in all drug cases solely because narcotics, by their very nature, are easily destroyed. More information is needed. The officers must have particular grounds to provide them with reasonable cause to believe that in the specific case at hand, drugs will be destroyed. This court stated that an allegation that drugs had been sold on the premises is inadequate to provide reason to believe that the evidence will be destroyed if the police announce their presence prior to the search.

Cleveland also stands for the proposition that the police cannot justify a no-knock entry by merely alleging that drug dealers are often armed, and hence, no-knock is necessary to protect the police and others. * * *

We now reexamine our holding[ ] in *Cleveland* * * *.

* * * [D]rugs may be destroyed easily. Several jurisdictions have acknowledged that most drugs are easily disposed of using standard plumbing. We now overrule *Cleveland* and find that the easily disposable nature of narcotics provides police with evidence sufficient to form a reasonable belief that no-knock entry is necessary to prevent the destruction of evidence.

* * * We * * * hold that, due to the destructibility of the evidence, a no-knock search is reasonable any time the police have a warrant, supported by probable cause, to search a residence for "evidence of drug dealing". Under these circumstances, the police may dispense with the rule of announcement. At least six other courts have adopted such a "blanket" exception to the rule of announcement.

Some courts have limited this no-knock exception to cases in which the police are searching for drugs kept in small quantities. These courts believe that packaging the narcotics in small amounts increases the likelihood that the occupants will be able to destroy the drugs if the police announce their entry. We reject this limitation to our newly adopted "blanket" exception to the rule of announcement. To allow the method of entry to be based on the packaging of the drugs would create a test without certainty.

* * *

Historically, the primary purpose of the rule of announcement was to decrease the potential for violence when the police execute a search warrant. The common belief has always been that the occupants of a home are less likely to react violently towards an intruder if the occupants are forewarned that the intruder is a police officer with a judicially issued warrant. On the other hand, if the police break into a home unannounced, the occupants are more likely to assume the intruder is a criminal—in which case the occupants may be justified in confronting the intruder with a weapon. In that case, the police are in turn more likely to respond with force against the occupants.

This rule of announcement rationale * * * is no longer valid in today's drug culture. In fact, by announcing their presence, police may actually increase the likelihood for violence. Due to * * * "systemic" violence aimed at the police and rival drug dealers, when the police execute * * * a search warrant, they may be putting themselves in more danger, rather than less, by announcing their presence before they enter.

Contrary to the historical notion that following the rule of announcement is more likely to prevent violence than executing a no-knock search, the opposite is more likely true. Police departments and commentators have determined that the police can decrease the possibility for violence during a search by taking control of the situation quickly. This can best be accomplished using an unannounced, dynamic entry. * * *

In cases like this, where the police have a valid warrant, supported by probable cause, to search a home for "evidence of drug dealing", the officers executing the warrant have the incentive to choose the safest method of entry. Hence, in such cases, we will yield to the police officers' discretion in choosing whether or not to follow the rule of announcement. We overrule *Cleveland* * * * and hold that when the police request a warrant to search for "evidence of drug dealing", due to the inherent violence associated with drug dealing, the police need not offer particularized evidence of weapons to demonstrate that exigent circumstances exist justifying a no-knock search.

State v. Stevens, 181 Wis.2d 410, 424–30, 511 N.W.2d 591, 595–97 (1994), cert. denied ___ U.S. ___, 115 S.Ct. 2245, ___ L.Ed.2d ___ (1995).

Chapter 4

DETENTIONS OF PERSONS AND RELATED SEARCHES

B. FIELD DETENTIONS AND RELATED SEARCHES

Page 230. Insert the following at the end of note 5 after Terry v. Ohio:

In California v. Hodari D., 499 U.S. 621, 111 S.Ct. 1547, 113 L.Ed.2d 690 (1991), two officers in street clothes but wearing jackets with "Police" embossed on both the front and back were driving on patrol in a high-crime area of Oakland, California. As they rounded a corner, they saw four or five youths huddled around a small red car parked at the curb. When the youths saw the officers' unmarked car approach, they "took flight." The red car pulled away at a high rate of speed. Could the officers stop one or more of the youths? Justice Scalia's opinion for the Court commented:

> That it would be unreasonable to stop, for brief inquiry, young men who scatter in panic upon the mere sighting of the police is not self-evident and arguably contradicts proverbial common sense. See Proverbs 28:1 ("The wicked flee when no man pursueth.") We do not decide that point here, [because the State conceded below that the officers did not have the "reasonable suspicion" necessary to stop the young men].

499 U.S. at 623 n. 1, 111 S.Ct. at 1549 n. 1, 113 L.Ed.2d at 695–96 n. 1.

Page 233. Insert the following case before Florida v. Royer:

MINNESOTA v. DICKERSON

Supreme Court of the United States, 1993.
___ U.S. ___, 113 S.Ct. 2130, 124 L.Ed.2d 334.

JUSTICE WHITE delivered the opinion of the Court.

In this case, we consider whether the Fourth Amendment permits the seizure of contraband detected through a police officer's sense of touch during a protective pat-down search.

I

On the evening of November 9, 1989, two Minneapolis police officers were patrolling an area on the city's north side in a marked squad car. At about 8:15 p.m., one of the officers observed respondent leaving a 12-unit apartment building on Morgan Avenue North. The officer, having previously responded to complaints of drug sales in the building's hallways and having executed several search warrants on the premises, considered the building to be a notorious "crack house." According to testimony credited by the trial court, respondent began walking toward the police but, upon spotting the squad car and making eye contact with one of the officers, abruptly halted and began walking in the opposite direction. His suspicion aroused, this officer watched as respondent turned and entered an alley on the other side of the apartment building. Based upon respondent's seemingly evasive actions and the fact that he had just left a building known for cocaine traffic, the officers decided to stop respondent and investigate further.

The officers pulled their squad car into the alley and ordered respondent to stop and submit to a patdown search. The search revealed no weapons, but the officer conducting the search did take an interest in a small lump in respondent's nylon jacket. The officer later testified: "[A]s I pat-searched the front of his body, I felt a lump, a small lump, in the front pocket. I examined it with my fingers and it slid and it felt to be a lump of crack cocaine in cellophane." The officer then reached into respondent's pocket and retrieved a small plastic bag containing one fifth of one gram of crack cocaine. Respondent was arrested and charged in Hennepin County District Court with possession of a controlled substance.

Before trial, respondent moved to suppress the cocaine. The trial court first concluded that the officers were justified under Terry v. Ohio, 392 U.S. 1, 88 S.Ct. 1868, 20 L.Ed.2d 889 (1968), in stopping respondent to investigate whether he might be engaged in criminal activity. The court further found that the officers were justified in frisking respondent to ensure that he was not carrying a weapon. Finally, analogizing to the "plain-view" doctrine, under which officers may make a warrantless seizure of contraband found in plain view during a lawful search for other items, the trial court ruled that the officers' seizure of the cocaine did not violate the Fourth Amendment:

> "To this Court there is no distinction as to which sensory perception the officer uses to conclude that the material is contraband. An experienced officer may rely upon his sense of smell in DWI stops or in recognizing the smell of burning marijuana in an automobile. The sound of a shotgun being racked would clearly support certain reactions by an officer. The sense of touch, grounded in experience and training, is as reliable as perceptions drawn from other senses. 'Plain feel,' therefore, is no different than plain view and will equally support the seizure here."

His suppression motion having failed, respondent proceeded to trial and was found guilty.

On appeal, the Minnesota Supreme Court affirmed [the intermediate court's reversal of the conviction]. * * * [T]he State Supreme Court held that both the stop and the frisk of respondent were valid under *Terry,* but found the seizure of the cocaine to be unconstitutional. The court expressly refused "to extend the plain view doctrine to the sense of touch" on the grounds that "the sense of touch is inherently less immediate and less reliable than the sense of sight" and that "the sense of touch is far more intrusive into the personal privacy that is at the core of the [F]ourth [A]mendment." The court thus appeared to adopt a categorical rule barring the seizure of any contraband detected by an officer through the sense of touch during a patdown search for weapons. The court further noted that "[e]ven if we recognized a 'plain feel' exception, the search in this case would not qualify" because "[t]he pat search of the defendant went far beyond what is permissible under *Terry.*" As the State Supreme Court read the record, the officer conducting the search ascertained that the lump in respondent's jacket was contraband only after probing and investigating what he certainly knew was not a weapon.

We granted certiorari to resolve a conflict among the state and federal courts over whether contraband detected through the sense of touch during a patdown search may be admitted into evidence. We now affirm.

II

A

* * * Time and again, this Court has observed that searches and seizures " 'conducted outside the judicial process, without prior approval by judge or magistrate, are per se unreasonable under the Fourth Amendment—subject only to a few specifically established and well delineated exceptions.' " Thompson v. Louisiana, 469 U.S. 17, 19–20, 105 S.Ct. 409, 410, 83 L.Ed.2d 246 (1984) (per curiam) (quoting Katz v. United States, 389 U.S. 347, 357, 88 S.Ct. 507, 514, 19 L.Ed.2d 576 (1967) (footnotes omitted)); Mincey v. Arizona, 437 U.S. 385, 390, 98 S.Ct. 2408, 2412, 57 L.Ed.2d 290 (1978); see also United States v. Place, 462 U.S. 696, 701, 103 S.Ct. 2637, 2641, 77 L.Ed.2d 110 (1983). One such exception was recognized in Terry v. Ohio, 392 U.S. 1, 88 S.Ct. 1868, 20 L.Ed.2d 889 (1968), which held that "where a police officer observes unusual conduct which leads him reasonably to conclude in light of his experience that criminal activity may be afoot" the officer may briefly stop the suspicious person and make "reasonable inquiries" aimed at confirming or dispelling his suspicions. Id., 392 U.S. at 30, 88 S.Ct. at 1884; see also Adams v. Williams, 407 U.S. 143, 145–146, 92 S.Ct. 1921, 1922–23, 32 L.Ed.2d 612 (1972).

Terry further held that "[w]hen an officer is justified in believing that the individual whose suspicious behavior he is investigating at close range is armed and presently dangerous to the officer or to others," the officer may conduct a patdown search "to determine whether the person is in fact carrying a weapon." "The purpose of this limited search is not to discover evidence of crime, but to allow the officer to pursue his investigation without fear of violence...." *Adams,* supra, at 146, 92 S.Ct. at 1923. Rather, a protective search—permitted without a warrant and on the basis of reasonable suspicion less than probable cause—must be strictly "limited to that which is necessary for the discovery of weapons which might be used to harm the officer or others nearby." If the protective search goes beyond what is necessary to determine if the suspect is armed, it is no longer valid under *Terry* and its fruits will be suppressed. Sibron v. New York, 392 U.S. 40, 65–66, 88 S.Ct. 1889, 1904, 20 L.Ed.2d 917 (1968).

These principles were settled 25 years ago when, on the same day, the Court announced its decisions in *Terry* and *Sibron*. The question presented today is whether police officers may seize nonthreatening contraband detected during a protective patdown search of the sort permitted by *Terry*. We think the answer is clearly that they may, so long as the officer's search stays within the bounds marked by *Terry*.

B

We have already held that police officers, at least under certain circumstances, may seize contraband detected during the lawful execution of a Terry search. In Michigan v. Long, [463 U.S. 1032, 103 S.Ct. 3469, 77 L.Ed.2d 1201 (1983)], for example, police approached a man who had driven his car into a ditch and who appeared to be under the influence of some intoxicant. As the man moved to reenter the car from the roadside, police spotted a knife on the floorboard. The officers stopped the man, subjected him to a patdown search, and then inspected the interior of the vehicle for other weapons. During the search of the passenger compartment, the police discovered an open pouch containing marijuana and seized it. This Court upheld the validity of the search and seizure under *Terry*. The Court held first that, in the context of a roadside encounter, where police have reasonable suspicion based on specific and articulable facts to believe that a driver may be armed and dangerous, they may conduct a protective search for weapons not only of the driver's person but also of the passenger compartment of the automobile. Of course, the protective search of the vehicle, being justified solely by the danger that weapons stored there could be used against the officers or bystanders, must be "limited to those areas in which a weapon may be placed or hidden." The Court then held: "If, while conducting a legitimate *Terry* search of the interior of the automobile, the officer should, as here, discover contraband other than weapons, he clearly cannot be required to ignore the contraband, and the Fourth Amendment does not require its suppression in such circumstances." Id., at 1050, 103 S.Ct. at 3481.

The Court in *Long* justified this latter holding by reference to our cases under the "plain-view" doctrine. Under that doctrine, if police are lawfully in a position from which they view an object, if its incriminating character is immediately apparent, and if the officers have a lawful right of access to the object, they may seize it without a warrant. If, however, the police lack probable cause to believe that an object in plain view is contraband without conducting some further search of the object—i.e., if "its incriminating character [is not] 'immediately apparent,' "—the plain-view doctrine cannot justify its seizure.

We think that this doctrine has an obvious application by analogy to cases in which an officer discovers contraband through the sense of touch during an otherwise lawful search. The rationale of the plain view doctrine is that if contraband is left in open view and is observed by a police officer from a lawful vantage point, there has been no invasion of a legitimate expectation of privacy and thus no "search" within the meaning of the Fourth Amendment—or at least no search independent of the initial intrusion that gave the officers their vantage point. The warrantless seizure of contraband that presents itself in this manner is deemed justified by the realization that resort to a neutral magistrate under such circumstances would often be impracticable and would do little to promote the objectives of the Fourth Amendment. The same can be said of tactile discoveries of contraband. If a police officer lawfully pats down a suspect's outer clothing and feels an object whose contour or mass makes its identity immediately apparent, there has been no invasion of the suspect's privacy beyond that already authorized by the officer's search for weapons; if the object is contraband, its warrantless seizure would be justified by the same practical considerations that inhere in the plain view context.

The Minnesota Supreme Court rejected an analogy to the plain-view doctrine on two grounds: first, its belief that "the sense of touch is inherently less immediate and less reliable than the sense of sight," and second, that "the sense of touch is far more intrusive into the personal privacy that is at the core of the [F]ourth [A]mendment." We have a somewhat different view. First, *Terry* itself demonstrates that the sense of touch is capable of revealing the nature of an object with sufficient reliability to support a seizure. The very premise of *Terry,* after all, is that officers will be able to detect the presence of weapons through the sense of touch and *Terry* upheld precisely such a seizure. Even if it were true that the sense of touch is generally less reliable than the sense of sight, that only suggests that officers will less often be able to justify seizures of unseen contraband. Regardless of whether the officer detects the contraband by sight or by touch, however, the Fourth Amendment's requirement that the officer have probable cause to believe that the item is contraband before seizing it ensures against excessively speculative seizures. The court's second concern—that touch is more intrusive into privacy than is sight—is inapposite in light of the fact that the intrusion the court fears has already been authorized by the lawful search for weapons. The seizure of an item whose identity is already known occasions no further invasion of privacy. Accordingly, the suspect's privacy interests are not advanced by a categorical rule barring the seizure of contraband plainly detected through the sense of touch.

III

It remains to apply these principles to the facts of this case. Respondent has not challenged the finding made by the trial court and affirmed by both the Court of Appeals and the State Supreme Court that the police were justified under *Terry* in stopping him and frisking him for weapons. Thus, the dispositive question before this Court is whether the officer who conducted the search was acting within the lawful bounds marked by *Terry* at the time he gained probable cause to believe that the lump in respondent's jacket was contraband. The State District Court did not make precise findings on this point, instead finding simply that the officer, after feeling "a small, hard object wrapped in plastic" in respondent's pocket, "formed the opinion that the object . . . was crack . . . cocaine." The District Court also noted that the officer made "no claim that he suspected this object to be a weapon," a finding affirmed on appeal. The Minnesota Supreme Court, after "a close examination of the record," held that the officer's own testimony "belies any notion that he 'immediately' " recognized the lump as crack cocaine. Rather, the court concluded, the officer determined that the lump was contraband only after "squeezing, sliding and otherwise manipulating the contents of the defendant's pocket"—a pocket which the officer already knew contained no weapon.

Under the State Supreme Court's interpretation of the record before it, it is clear that the court was correct in holding that the police officer in this case overstepped the bounds of the "strictly circumscribed" search for weapons allowed under *Terry*. Where, as here, "an officer who is executing a valid search for one item seizes a different item," this Court rightly "has been sensitive to the danger . . . that officers will enlarge a specific authorization, furnished by a warrant or an exigency, into the equivalent of a general warrant to rummage and seize at will." Texas v. Brown, 460 U.S. [730,] 748, 103 S.Ct. [1535,] 1546–47[, 75 L.Ed.2d 502] [(1983)] (Stevens, J., concurring in judgment). Here, the officer's continued exploration of respondent's pocket after having concluded that it contained no weapon was unrelated to "[t]he sole justification of the search [under *Terry:*] . . . the protection of the police officer and others nearby." It therefore amounted to the sort of evidentiary search that *Terry* expressly refused to authorize, and that we have condemned in subsequent cases.

* * * Although the officer was lawfully in a position to feel the lump in respondent's pocket, because *Terry* entitled him to place his hands upon respondent's jacket, the court below determined that the incriminating character of the object was not immediately apparent to him. Rather, the officer determined that the item was contraband only after conducting a further search, one not authorized by *Terry* or by any other exception to the warrant requirement. Because this further search of respondent's pocket was constitutionally invalid, the seizure of the cocaine that followed is likewise unconstitutional.

IV

For these reasons, the judgment of the Minnesota Supreme Court is

Affirmed.

JUSTICE SCALIA, concurring.

I take it to be a fundamental principle of constitutional adjudication that the terms in the Constitution must be given the meaning ascribed to them at the time of their ratification. Thus, when the Fourth Amendment provides that "[t]he right of the people to be secure in their persons, houses, papers, and effects, against unreasonable searches and seizures, shall not be violated" (emphasis added), it "is to be construed in the light of what was deemed an unreasonable search and seizure when it was adopted," Carroll v. United States, 267 U.S. 132, 149, 45 S.Ct. 280, 284, 69 L.Ed.2d 543 (1925). * * *

My problem with the present case is that I am not entirely sure that the physical search—the "frisk"—that produced the evidence at issue here complied with that constitutional standard. The decision of ours that gave approval to such searches, Terry v. Ohio, 392 U.S. 1, 88 S.Ct. 1868, 20 L.Ed.2d 889 (1968), made no serious attempt to determine compliance with traditional standards, but rather, according to the style of this Court at the time, simply adjudged that such a search was "reasonable" by current estimations.

There is good evidence, I think, that the "stop" portion of the *Terry* "stop-and-frisk" holding accords with the common law—that it had long been considered reasonable to detain suspicious persons for the purpose of demanding that they give an account of themselves. * * *

I am unaware, however, of any precedent for a physical search of a person thus temporarily detained for questioning. * * *

I frankly doubt, moreover, whether the fiercely proud men who adopted our Fourth Amendment would have allowed themselves to be subjected, on mere suspicion of being armed and dangerous, to such indignity—which is described as follows in a police manual:

> "Check the subject's neck and collar. A check should be made under the subject's arm. Next a check should be made of the upper back. The lower back should also be checked.
>
> "A check should be made of the upper part of the man's chest and the lower region around the stomach. The belt, a favorite concealment spot, should be checked. The inside thigh and crotch area also should be searched. The legs should be checked for possible weapons. The last items to be checked are the shoes and cuffs of the subject." J. Moynahan, Police Searching Procedures 7 (1963) (citations omitted).

On the other hand, even if a "frisk" prior to arrest would have been considered impermissible in 1791, perhaps it was considered permissible by 1868, when the Fourteenth Amendment (the basis for applying the Fourth Amendment to the States) was adopted. Or perhaps it is only since that time that concealed weapons capable of harming the interrogator quickly and from beyond arm's reach have become common—which might alter the judgment of what is "reasonable" under the original standard. But technological changes were no more discussed in *Terry* than was the original state of the law.

* * * [T]hough I do not favor the mode of analysis in *Terry,* I cannot say that its result was wrong. Constitutionality of the "frisk" in the present case was neither challenged nor argued. Assuming, therefore, that the search was lawful, I agree with the Court's premise that any evidence incidentally discovered in the course of it would be admissible, and join the Court's opinion in its entirety.

CHIEF JUSTICE REHNQUIST, with whom JUSTICE BLACKMUN and JUSTICE THOMAS join, concurring in part and dissenting in part.

I join Parts I and II of the Court's opinion. Unlike the Court, however, I would vacate the judgment of the Supreme Court of Minnesota and remand the case to that court for further proceedings.

The Court, correctly in my view, states that "the dispositive question before this Court is whether the officer who conducted the search was acting within the lawful bounds marked by Terry [v. Ohio, 392 U.S. 1, 88 S.Ct. 1868, 20 L.Ed.2d 889 (1968),] at the time he gained probable cause to believe that the lump in respondent's jacket was contraband." The Court then goes on to point out that the state trial court did not make precise findings on this point, but accepts the appellate findings made by the Supreme Court of Minnesota. I believe that these findings, like those of the trial court, are imprecise and not directed expressly to the question of the officer's probable cause to believe that the lump was contraband. Because the Supreme Court of Minnesota employed a Fourth Amendment analysis which differs significantly from that now adopted by this Court, I would vacate its judgment and remand the case for further proceedings there in the light of this Court's opinion.

Page 239. Insert the following new notes after Florida v. Royer:

1a. Although meeting the requirement applied in *Chesternut* is a *necessary* condition for a seizure, it is not always *sufficient* to establish that a seizure occurred. In California v. Hodari D., 499 U.S. 621, 111 S.Ct. 1547, 113 L.Ed.2d 690 (1991), Officer Pertoso and his partner were on a patrol in a high-crime rate area. Although they were dressed in street clothes and the car was unmarked, they wore jackets with "Police" embossed on the front and back. Four or five youths, including Hodari, huddled around a parked car saw the officers' car approach and took flight. Pertoso alighted and pursued Hodari. Just before Pertoso caught Hodari, Hodari realized the officer was behind him and tossed away what appeared to be a small rock. Moments later, Pertoso tackled Hodari and handcuffed him. The item Hodari had discarded was retrieved and turned out to be crack cocaine. Hodari's motion to suppress the cocaine was denied by the trial court but a state appellate court reversed, reasoning that the cocaine's discovery was the fruit of an illegal seizure of Hodari by Pertoso.

The Supreme Court assumed that Pertoso lacked reasonable suspicion and addressed only whether at the time he dropped the cocaine, Hodari had been "seized" by Pertoso. A majority held he had not. Justice Scalia's opinion agreed that a seizure occurs when an officer, "by means of physical force or show of authority, has in some way restrained the liberty of a citizen." Pertoso had applied no physical force to Hodari and therefore could have "seized" him only by a "show of authority." Justice Scalia explained:

> The narrow question before us is whether, with respect to a show of authority * * *, a seizure occurs even though the suspect does not yield. We hold that it does not.
>
> The language of the Fourth Amendment, of course, cannot sustain [Hodari's] contention. The word "seizure" readily bears the meaning of a laying on of hands or application of physical force to restrain movement, even when it is ultimately unsuccessful. ("She seized the purse-snatcher, but he broke out of her grasp.") It does not remotely apply, however, to the prospect of a policeman yelling "Stop, in the name of the law!" at a fleeing form that continues to flee. That is no seizure. * * * An arrest [at common law] requires *either* physical force * * * *or,* where that is absent, submission to the assertion of authority.
>
> We do not think it desirable, even as a policy matter, to stretch the Fourth Amendment beyond its words and beyond the meaning of arrest * * *. Street pursuits always place the public at some risk, and compliance with police orders to stop should therefore be encouraged. Only a few of these orders, we must presume, will be without adequate basis, and since the addressee has no ready means of identifying the deficient ones it almost invariably is the responsible course to comply. Unlawful orders will not be deterred, moreover, by sanctioning through the exclusionary rule those of them that are *not* obeyed. Since policemen do not command "Stop!" expecting to be ignored, or give chase hoping to be outrun, it fully suffices to apply the deterrent to their genuine, successful seizures.
>
> * * *
>
> In sum, assuming that Pertoso's pursuit in the present case constituted a "show of authority" enjoining Hodari to halt, since Hodari did not comply with that injunction he was not seized until he was tackled. The cocaine abandoned while he was running was in this case not the fruit of a seizure, and his motion to exclude evidence of it was properly denied.

499 U.S. at 626–29, 111 S.Ct. at 1550–52, 113 L.Ed.2d at 697–99.

Justice Scalia had earlier noted that at common law "the mere grasping or application of physical force with lawful authority, whether or not it succeeded in subduing the arrestee, was sufficient [to constitute an arrest]." His discussion seemed to incorporate that into the definition of "seizure;" in the portion of the opinion quoted above he referred to "a laying on of hands." Does this mean that if before Hodari had thrown the cocaine Pertoso's outstretched hand had brushed the rearmost part of Hodari's body, Pertoso would have "seized" Hodari? With regard to a related matter, Justice Scalia commented:

> To say that an arrest is effected by the slightest application of physical force, despite the arrestee's escape, is not to say that for Fourth Amendment purposes there is a *continuing* arrest during that period. If, for example, Pertoso had laid his hands upon Hodari to arrest him, but Hodari had broke away and had *then* cast away the cocaine, it would hardly be realistic to say that disclosure had been made during the course of an arrest.

499 U.S. at 624, 111 S.Ct. at 1550, 113 L.Ed.2d at 696–97.

Justice Stevens, joined by Justice Marshall, dissented, criticizing the majority's reliance upon the common law of arrest in defining "seizure." Earlier case law, including *Royer* and *Chesternut,* had accepted that a seizure occurs whenever a reasonable person feels unfree to leave, he argued, and this should remain the standard. He speculated as to the impact of the majority's approach:

> If an officer decides to make [a constitutionally-prohibited] random stop [of a car to determine if the driver has a valid driver's license] and, after flashing his lights, but before the vehicle comes to a complete stop, sees that the license plate has expired, can he justify his action on the ground that the seizure became lawful after it was initiated but before it was completed? In an airport setting, may a drug enforcement agent now approach a group of passengers with his gun drawn, announce a "baggage search," and rely on the passengers' reaction to justify his investigative stops?

499 U.S. at 1561, 111 S.Ct. at 1561, 113 L.Ed.2d at 710 (Stevens, J., dissenting). He added:

> It is too early to know the consequences of the Court's holding. If carried to its logical conclusion, it will encourage unlawful displays of force that will frighten countless innocent citizens into surrendering whatever privacy rights they may still have.

499 U.S. at 646–47, 111 S.Ct. at 1561, 113 L.Ed.2d at 710.

1b. The law enforcement practice of "bus sweeps" was at issue in Florida v. Bostick, 501 U.S. 429, 111 S.Ct. 2382, 115 L.Ed.2d 389 (1991). Bostick was prosecuted for possession of cocaine found in his luggage; his motion to suppress the cocaine was overruled. The basic facts were as follows:

> Two officers, complete with badges, insignia and one of them holding a recognizable zipper pouch, containing a pistol, boarded a bus bound from Miami to Atlanta during a stopover in Fort Lauderdale. Eyeing the passengers, the officers admittedly without articulable suspicion, picked out the defendant passenger and asked to inspect his ticket and identification. The ticket, from Miami to Atlanta, matched the defendant's identification and both were immediately returned to him as unremarkable. However, the two police officers persisted and explained their presence as narcotics agents on the lookout for illegal drugs. In pursuit of that aim, they then requested the defendant's consent to search his luggage.

501 U.S. at 431–32, 111 S.Ct. at 2384–85, 115 L.Ed.2d at 396, quoting 554 So.2d 1153, 1154–1155 (Fla.1989). Although the testimony was conflicting, the trial court implicitly found that the officers advised Bostick that he had a right to refuse the consent and that he nevertheless consented to a search of the bag in which the cocaine was found.

A majority of the Supreme Court construed the Florida Supreme Court's holding as adopting a *per se* rule that officers who board buses during scheduled stops to question passengers and to seek consent for luggage searches necessarily "seize" the passengers confronted. If the officers lack reasonable suspicion, the seizure is unreasonable and taints the subsequently-given consent. In so adopting a *per se* rule, the Court held, the Florida court erred. As in other situations, a seizure does not necessarily occur simply because an officer approaches a bus passenger and asks a few questions. Whether on the facts of *Bostick* a seizure took place, the Court observed, was in "some doubt," and it remanded the case for the state courts to address that question under the correct legal standard. That standard, it continued, requires that in the context presented the state courts not focus upon whether Bostick felt "free to leave":

> When police attempt to question a person who is walking down the street or through an airport lobby, it makes sense to inquire whether a reasonable person would feel free to continue walking. But when the person is seated on a bus and has no desire to leave, the degree to which a reasonable person would feel that he or she could leave is not an accurate measure of the coercive effect of the encounter. * * * In such a situation, the appropriate inquiry is whether a reasonable person would feel free to decline the officers' requests or otherwise terminate the encounter. This formulation follows logically from prior cases and breaks no new ground. We have said before that the crucial test is whether, taking into account all of the circumstances surrounding the encounter, the police conduct would "have communicated to a reasonable person that he was not at liberty to ignore the police presence and go about his business." Where the encounter takes place is one factor, but it is not the only one. And * * * an individual may decline an officer's request without fearing prosecution. We have consistently held that a refusal to cooperate, without more, does not furnish the minimal level of objective justification needed for a detention or seizure.

501 U.S. at 435–37, 111 S.Ct. at 2387, 115 L.Ed.2d at 399–400. The majority added:

> We * * * reject * * * Bostick's argument that he must have been seized because no reasonable person would freely consent to a search of luggage that he or she knows contains drugs. This argument cannot prevail because the "reasonable person" test presupposes an *innocent* person.

501 U.S. at 437–38, 111 S.Ct. at 2388, 115 L.Ed.2d at 400.

Justice Marshall, joined by Justices Blackmun and Stevens, dissented. He declined to disagree with the majority's formulation of the test for determining whether a suspicionless bus sweep amounts to a Fourth Amendment "seizure." But he read the Florida court's holding as a finding that on the circumstances of the case that Bostick had been seized and he found this supported by the record. Bostick reasonably believed he was not free to terminate the encounter with the officers because he had no realistic alternatives. Remaining seated and refusing to respond to the questions, he suggested, could—given the officers' "intimidating show of authority"—have been viewed by Bostick as likely only to arouse the officers' suspicions and intensify their efforts. Bostick could not have known that under the law the officers could not hold his refusal to cooperate against him. Leaving, on the other hand, would have required squeezing past a "gunwielding inquisitor" blocking the bus aisle, and thus could have been regarded as unavailable as a practical option. Thus under the majority's standards, he concluded, the state court properly found a seizure which was unreasonable because reasonable suspicion was lacking. 501 U.S. at 444–50, 111 S.Ct. at 2391–95, 115 L.Ed.2d at 405–09 (Marshall, J., dissenting).

On remand, the Florida Supreme Court summarily approved the earlier decision of the intermediate appellate court affirming Bostick's conviction. Bostick v. State, 593 So.2d 494 (Fla.1992) (per curiam). The intermediate court had issued no opinion explaining its decision. Justice Barkett, joined by two other members of the court, dissented from the Florida Supreme Court's action. He reasoned that on the facts the officers seized Bostick:

> [U]nder the facts presented here, a reasonable person would not have felt free to ignore the police or decline to consent to a search. This was not a casual encounter on a street corner where a reasonable person might feel free to treat the police like an encounter with any other citizen, i.e., to ignore them, refuse to converse with them, or simply to walk away. * * * [U]nder certain circumstances, a reasonable person may feel free to terminate an encounter with the police when confronted in the confines of a bus, but I do not find those circumstances to exist here.

593 So.2d at 495–96 (Barkett, J., dissenting).

C. TRAFFIC "STOPS," SOBRIETY CHECKPOINTS, AND RELATED DETENTIONS

Page 258. Insert the following new Note after Michigan v. Sitz:

NOTE

On remand, the Michigan courts held that the roadblock at issue violated the Michigan Constitution's prohibition against unreasonable searches and seizures. Sitz v. Department of State Police, 443 Mich. 744, 506 N.W.2d 209 (1993), affirming 193 Mich.App. 690, 485 N.W.2d 135 (1992). After reviewing its case law, the Michigan Supreme Court explained:

> [T]he history of our jurisprudence conclusively demonstrates that, in the context of automobile seizures, we have extended more expansive protection to our citizens than that extended in *Sitz.* This Court has never recognized the right of the state, without any level of suspicion whatsoever, to detain members of the population at large for criminal investigatory purposes. Nor has Michigan completely acquiesced to the judgment of "politically accountable officials when determining reasonableness in such a context. * * *
>
> We do not suggest that in a different context we might not reach a similar result under the balancing test of reasonableness employed in *Sitz.* Indeed, our precedent regarding automobiles implicitly incorporates a balancing test that is inherent in assessing the reasonableness of warrantless searches or seizures. We hold only that the protection afforded to the seizure of vehicles for criminal investigatory purposes has both an historical foundation and a contemporary justification that is not outweighed by the necessity advanced. Suspicionless criminal investigatory seizures, and extreme deference to the judgment of politically accountable officials is, in this context, contrary to Michigan constitutional precedent.

443 Mich. at 776–79, 506 N.W.2d at 223–25.

Chapter 5

"WARRANTLESS" SEARCHES

A. THE EMERGENCY DOCTRINE

Page 275. Insert the following at the end of note 5 following Vale v. Louisiana:

On remand in *Buie,* a split Maryland court upheld the sweep. Buie v. State, 320 Md. 696, 580 A.2d 167 (1990) (plurality opinion), cert. denied 498 U.S. 1106, 111 S.Ct. 1011, 112 L.Ed.2d 1094 (1991). Is it necessary under *Buie* for the officers who make the sweep to subjectively believe that the area swept harbors a person posing a danger to the officers? A plurality of the Maryland court read *Buie* as imposing no such requirement and as demanding only that the situation be one in which a reasonable officer could form such a belief:

> We conclude that in determining the existence of reasonable suspicion in a case such as this, the objective standard must be used. * * * The experience and training of the particular police officers involved will form a part of the matrix of facts that define the circumstances which must be considered, but the test is whether a reasonably prudent police officer, under those circumstances, is justified in forming a reasonable suspicion that the house is harboring a person posing danger to those on the arrest scene.

320 Md. at 701, 580 A.2d at 170. It added:

> We need not here consider whether proof by the defendant that an officer undertook a search in bad faith, i.e., believing he had no right to do so, would result in suppression of the fruits of a search that was objectively reasonable. There is no evidence of bad faith in this case. * * *

320 Md. at 701 n. 1, 580 A.2d at 170 n. 1.

The plurality was apparently concerned that if the State needed to prove that the officers subjectively believed that there was a dangerous individual in the basement, the State's proof might fail. When the detective was asked why he went in the basement, he responded "in case there was someone else in the basement." The dissent pointed out that the detective was asked by defense counsel whether he was "worried about there being any danger or anything like that," and the detective replied in the negative. But having adopted a purely objective approach, the plurality explained its result by concluding that a prudent police officer in the detective's position could reasonably have suspected that the basement harbored an individual who posed a danger to those on the arrest scene and thus the detective was justified in conducting a cursory sweep of that area to neutralize the danger.

C. CONSENT SEARCHES

Page 316. Insert the following Note after Illinois v. Rodriguez:

NOTE

On remand, the Illinois Appellate Court remanded the case to the trial court for a factual hearing. The trial judge noted that Rodriguez had not been in further "trouble," and suggested that the State reduce the charge. This was done and Rodriguez pleaded guilty. Therefore, the admissibility of the evidence seized during the search of the apartment was not further considered. Interview with James W. Reilly, counsel for Edward Rodriguez.

Page 316. Insert the following new subsection after Illinois v. Rodriguez:

3. SCOPE OF CONSENT

If effective consent was given by a person with authority to provide such consent, problems may still be presented by the scope of that consent. How extensive and intrusive a search is supported by particular words of consent? How should a court approach the task of construing words that constitute consent to a search of some sort? The Supreme Court addressed these issues in the principal case.

FLORIDA v. JIMENO

Supreme Court of the United States, 1991.
500 U.S. 248, 111 S.Ct. 1801, 114 L.Ed.2d 297.

CHIEF JUSTICE REHNQUIST delivered the opinion of the Court.

* * *

This case began when a Dade County police officer, Frank Trujillo, overheard respondent, Enio Jimeno, arranging what appeared to be a drug transaction over a public telephone. Believing that respondent might be involved in illegal drug trafficking, Officer Trujillo followed his car. The officer observed respondent make a right turn at a red light without stopping. He then pulled respondent over to the side of the road in order to issue him a traffic citation. Officer Trujillo told respondent that he had been stopped for committing a traffic infraction. The officer went on to say that he had reason to believe that respondent was carrying narcotics in his car, and asked permission to search the car. He explained that respondent did not have to consent to a search of the car. Respondent stated that he had nothing to hide, and gave Trujillo permission to search the automobile. After two passengers stepped out of respondent's car, Officer Trujillo went to the passenger side, opened the door, and saw a folded, brown paper bag on the floorboard. The officer picked up the bag, opened it, and found a kilogram of cocaine inside.

Respondent was charged with possession with intent to distribute cocaine in violation of Florida law. Before trial, he moved to suppress the cocaine found in the bag on the ground that his consent to search the car did not extend to the closed paper bag inside of the car. The trial court granted the motion. It found that although respondent "could have assumed that the officer would have searched the bag" at the time he gave his consent, his mere consent to search the car did not carry with it specific consent to open the bag and examine its contents.

The Florida District Court of Appeal affirmed the trial court's decision to suppress the evidence of the cocaine. In doing so, the court established a *per se* rule that "consent to a general search for narcotics does not extend to 'sealed containers within the general area agreed to by the defendant.'" The Florida Supreme Court affirmed, relying upon its decision in State v. Wells, 539 So.2d 464 (1989) aff'd on other grounds, 495 U.S. 1, 110 S.Ct. 1632, 109 L.Ed.2d 1 (1990). We granted certiorari to determine whether consent to search a vehicle may extend to closed containers found inside the vehicle * * * and we now reverse the judgment of the Supreme Court of Florida.

The touchstone of the Fourth Amendment is reasonableness. The Fourth Amendment does not proscribe all state-initiated searches and seizures; it merely proscribes those which are unreasonable. Thus, we have long approved consensual searches because it is no doubt reasonable for the police to conduct a search once they have been permitted to do so. Schneckloth v. Bustamonte, 412 U.S. 218, 219, 93 S.Ct. 2041, 3043–44, 36 L.Ed.2d 854 (1973). The standard for measuring the scope of a suspect's consent under the Fourth Amendment is that of "objective" reasonableness—what would the typical reasonable person have understood by the exchange between the officer and the suspect? Illinois v. Rodriguez, [497 U.S. 177, 110 S.Ct. 2793, 2798–2802, 111 L.Ed.2d 148 (1990)]. The question before us, then, is whether it is reasonable for an officer to consider a suspect's general consent to a search of his car to include consent to examine a paper bag lying on the floor of the car. We think that it is.

The scope of a search is generally defined by its expressed object. In this case, the terms of the search's authorization were simple. Respondent granted Officer Trujillo permission to search his car, and did not place any explicit limitation on the scope of the search. Trujillo had informed respondent that he believed respondent was carrying narcotics, and that he would be looking for narcotics in the car. We think that it was objectively reasonable for the police to conclude that the general consent to search respondent's car included consent to search containers within that car which might bear drugs. A reasonable person may be expected to know that narcotics are generally carried in some form of a container. "Contraband goods rarely are strewn across the trunk or floor of a car." The authorization to search in this case, therefore, extended beyond the surfaces of the car's interior to the paper bag lying on the car's floor.

The facts of this case are therefore different from those in State v. Wells, supra, on which the Supreme Court of Florida relied in affirming the suppression order in this case. There the Supreme Court of Florida held that consent to search the trunk of a car did not include authorization to pry open a locked briefcase found inside the trunk. It is very likely unreasonable to think that a suspect, by consenting to the search of his trunk, has agreed to the breaking open of a locked briefcase within the trunk, but it is otherwise with respect to a closed paper bag.

Respondent argues, and the Florida trial court agreed with him, that if the police wish to search closed containers within a car they must separately request permission to search each container. But we see no basis for adding this sort of superstructure to the Fourth Amendment's basic test of objective reasonableness. A suspect may of course delimit as he chooses the scope of the search to which he consents. But if his consent would reasonably be understood to extend to a particular container, the Fourth Amendment provides no grounds for requiring a more explicit authorization. "[T]he community has a real interest in encouraging consent, for the resulting search may yield necessary evidence for the solution and prosecution of crime, evidence that may ensure that a wholly innocent person is not wrongly charged with a criminal offense." Schneckloth v. Bustamonte, supra, 412 U.S. at 243, 93 S.Ct. at 2056.

The judgment of the Supreme Court of Florida is accordingly reversed, and the case remanded for further proceedings not inconsistent with this opinion.

It is so ordered.

JUSTICE MARSHALL, with whom JUSTICE STEVENS joins, dissenting.

[A]nalysis of this question must start by identifying the differing expectations of privacy that attach to cars and closed containers. It is well established that an individual has but a limited expectation of privacy in the interior of his car. * * * In contrast, it is equally well established that an individual has a heightened expectation of privacy in the contents of a closed container. Luggage, handbags, paper bags, and other containers are common repositories for one's papers and effects, and the protection of these items from state intrusion lies at the heart of the Fourth Amendment. * * *

The distinct privacy expectations that a person has in a car as opposed to a closed container do not merge when the individual uses his car to transport the container. * * *

Because an individual's expectation of privacy in a container is distinct from, and far greater than, his expectation of privacy in the interior of his car, it follows that an individual's consent to a search of the interior of his car cannot necessarily be understood as extending to containers in the car. At the very least, general consent to search the car is ambiguous with respect to containers found inside the car. In my view, the independent and divisible nature of the privacy interests in cars and containers mandates that a police officer who wishes to search a suspicious container found during a consensual automobile search obtain additional consent to search the container. If the driver intended to authorize search of the container, he will say so; if not, then he will say no.[1] The only objection that the police could have to such a rule is that it would prevent them from exploiting the ignorance of a citizen who simply did not anticipate that his consent to search the car would be understood to authorize the police to rummage through his packages.

* * *

I dissent.

NOTE

On remand, State v. Jimeno, 588 So.2d 233 (Fla.1991), Jimeno urged the Florida Supreme Court to construe the search at issue as unreasonable under the Florida constitution. The court declined, regarding itself as precluded by Article I, section 12 of the Florida Constitution:

> The right of the people to be secure in their persons, houses, papers and effects against unreasonable searches and seizures, and against the unreasonable interception of private communications by any means, shall not be violated. No warrant shall be issued except upon probable cause, supported by affidavit, particularly describing the place or places to be searched, the person or persons, thing or things to be seized, the communication to be intercepted, and the nature of evidence to be obtained. This right shall be construed in conformity with the 4th Amendment to the United States Constitution, as interpreted by the United States Supreme Court. Articles or information obtained in violation of this right shall not be admissible in evidence if such articles or information would be inadmissible under decisions of the United States Supreme Court construing the 4th Amendment to the United States Constitution.

D. AUTOMOBILE SEARCHES AND SEIZURES

2. SEARCHES OF CONTAINERS

Page 344. Add the following new case after United States v. Ross:

CALIFORNIA v. ACEVEDO

Supreme Court of the United States, 1991.
500 U.S. 565, 111 S.Ct. 1982, 114 L.Ed.2d 619.

JUSTICE BLACKMUN delivered the opinion of the Court.

This case requires us once again to consider the so-called "automobile exception" to the warrant requirement of the Fourth Amendment

[1] Alternatively, the police could obtain such consent in advance by asking the individual for permission to search both the car and any closed containers found inside.

and its application to the search of a closed container in the trunk of a car.

I

On October 28, 1987, Officer Coleman of the Santa Ana, Cal., Police Department received a telephone call from a federal drug enforcement agent in Hawaii. The agent informed Coleman that he had seized a package containing marijuana which was to have been delivered to the Federal Express Office in Santa Ana and which was addressed to J.R. Daza at 805 West Stevens Avenue in that city. The agent arranged to send the package to Coleman instead. Coleman then was to take the package to the Federal Express office and arrest the person who arrived to claim it.

Coleman received the package on October 29, verified its contents, and took it to the Senior Operations Manager at the Federal Express office. At about 10:30 a.m. on October 30, a man, who identified himself as Jamie Daza, arrived to claim the package. He accepted it and drove to his apartment on West Stevens. He carried the package into the apartment.

At 11:45 a.m., officers observed Daza leave the apartment and drop the box and paper that had contained the marijuana into a trash bin. Coleman at that point left the scene to get a search warrant. About 12:05 p.m., the officers saw Richard St. George leave the apartment carrying a blue knapsack which appeared to be half full. The officers stopped him as he was driving off, searched the knapsack, and found 1½ pounds of marijuana.

At 12:30 p.m., respondent Charles Steven Acevedo arrived. He entered Daza's apartment, stayed for about 10 minutes, and reappeared carrying a brown paper bag that looked full. The officers noticed that the bag was the size of one of the wrapped marijuana packages sent from Hawaii. Acevedo walked to a silver Honda in the parking lot. He placed the bag in the trunk of the car and started to drive away. Fearing the loss of evidence, officers in a marked police car stopped him. They opened the trunk and the bag, and found marijuana.

Respondent was charged in state court with possession of marijuana for sale * * *. He moved to suppress the marijuana found in the car. The motion was denied. He then pleaded guilty but appealed the denial of the suppression motion.

The California Court of Appeal, Fourth District, concluded that the marijuana found in the paper bag in the car's trunk should have been suppressed. * * *

The Supreme Court of California denied the State's petition for review. * * *

We granted certiorari to reexamine the law applicable to a closed container in an automobile, a subject that has troubled courts and law enforcement officers since it was first considered in *Chadwick*.

III

* * *

* * * We now must decide the question deferred in [United States v.] Ross[, 456 U.S. 798, 102 S.Ct. 2157, 72 L.Ed.2d 572 (1982)]: whether the Fourth Amendment requires the police to obtain a warrant to open the sack in a movable vehicle simply because they lack probable cause to search the entire car. We conclude that it does not.

IV

Dissenters in *Ross* asked why the suitcase in [Arkansas v.] Sanders[, 442 U.S. 753, 99 S.Ct. 2586, 61 L.Ed.2d 235 (1979)] was "more private, less difficult for police to seize and store, or in any other relevant respect more properly subject to the warrant requirement, than a container that police discover in a probable-cause search of an entire automobile?" We now agree that a container found after a general search of the automobile and a container found in a car after a limited search for the container are equally easy for the police to store and for the suspect to hide or destroy. In fact, we see no principled distinction in terms of either the privacy expectation or the exigent circumstances between the paper bag found by the police in *Ross* and the paper bag found by the police here. Furthermore, by attempting to distinguish between a container for which the police are specifically searching and a container which they come across in a car, we have provided only minimal protection for privacy and have impeded effective law enforcement.

The line between probable cause to search a vehicle and probable cause to search a package in that vehicle is not always clear, and separate rules that govern the two objects to be searched may enable the police to broaden their power to make warrantless searches and disserve privacy interests. We noted this in *Ross* in the context of a search of an entire vehicle. Recognizing that under Carroll [v. United States, 267 U.S. 132, 45 S.Ct. 280, 69 L.Ed. 543 (1925)], the "entire vehicle itself . . . could be searched without a warrant," we concluded that "prohibiting police from opening immediately a container in which the object of the search is most likely to be found and instead forcing them first to comb the entire vehicle would actually exacerbate the intrusion on privacy interests." At the moment when officers stop an automobile, it may be less than clear whether they suspect with a high degree of certainty that the vehicle contains drugs in a bag or simply contains drugs. If the police know that they may open a bag only if they are actually searching the entire car, they may search more extensively than they otherwise would in order to establish the general probable cause required by *Ross.*

To the extent that the *Chadwick–Sanders* rule protects privacy, its protection is minimal. Law enforcement officers may seize a container and hold it until they obtain a search warrant. "Since the police, by hypothesis, have probable cause to seize the property, we can assume that a warrant will be routinely forthcoming in the overwhelming majority of cases." *Sanders,* 442 U.S., at 770, 99 S.Ct. at 2596 (dissenting opinion). And the police often will be able to search containers without a warrant, despite the *Chadwick–Sanders* rule, as a search incident to a lawful arrest. * * *

Finally, the search of a paper bag intrudes far less on individual privacy than does the incursion sanctioned long ago in *Carroll.* In that case, prohibition agents slashed the upholstery of the automobile. This Court nonetheless found their search to be reasonable under the Fourth Amendment. If destroying the interior of an automobile is not unreasonable, we cannot conclude that looking inside a closed container is. In light of the minimal protection to privacy afforded by the *Chadwick–Sanders* rule, and our serious doubt whether that rule substantially serves privacy interests, we now hold that the Fourth Amendment does not compel separate treatment for an automobile search that extends only to a container within the vehicle.

V

The *Chadwick–Sanders* rule not only has failed to protect privacy but it has also confused courts and police officers and impeded effective law enforcement. The conflict between the *Carroll* doctrine cases and the *Chadwick–Sanders* line has been criticized in academic commentary. * * *

The discrepancy between the two rules has led to confusion for law enforcement officers. For example, when an officer, who has developed probable cause to believe that a vehicle contains drugs, begins to search the vehicle and immediately discovers a closed container, which rule applies? The defendant will argue that the fact that the officer first chose to search the container indicates that his probable cause extended only to the container and that *Chadwick* and *Sanders* therefore require a warrant. On the other hand, the fact that the officer first chose to search in the most obvious location should not restrict the propriety of the search. The *Chadwick* rule, as applied in *Sanders,* has devolved into an anomaly such that the more likely the police are to discover drugs in a container, the less authority they have to search it. We have noted the virtue of providing " 'clear and unequivocal' guidelines to the law enforcement profession." The *Chadwick–Sanders* rule is the antithesis of a " 'clear and unequivocal' guideline."

* * *

VI

The interpretation of the *Carroll* doctrine set forth in *Ross* now applies to all searches of containers found in an automobile. In other words, the police may search without a warrant if their search is supported by probable cause. The Court in *Ross* put it this way:

> "The scope of a warrantless search of an automobile ... is not defined by the nature of the container in which the contraband is secreted. Rather, it is defined by the object of the search and the places in which there is probable cause to believe that it may be found." 456 U.S., at 824, 102 S.Ct. at 2172.

It went on to note: "Probable cause to believe that a container placed in the trunk of a taxi contains contraband or evidence does not justify a search of the entire cab." Ibid. We reaffirm that principle. In the case before us, the police had probable cause to believe that the paper bag in the automobile's trunk contained marijuana. That probable cause now allows a warrantless search of the paper bag. The facts in the record reveal that the police did not have probable cause to believe that contraband was hidden in any other part of the automobile and a search of the entire vehicle would have been without probable cause and unreasonable under the Fourth Amendment.

* * *

Until today, this Court has drawn a curious line between the search of an automobile that coincidentally turns up a container and the search of a container that coincidentally turns up in an automobile. The protections of the Fourth Amendment must not turn on such coincidences. We therefore interpret *Carroll* as providing one rule to govern all automobile searches. The police may search an automobile and the containers within it where they have probable cause to believe contraband or evidence is contained.

The judgment of the California Court of Appeal is reversed and the case is remanded to that court for further proceedings not inconsistent with this opinion.

It is so ordered.

JUSTICE SCALIA, concurring in the judgment.

I agree with the dissent that it is anomalous for a briefcase to be protected by the "general requirement" of a prior warrant when it is being carried along the street, but for that same briefcase to become unprotected as soon as it is carried into an automobile. On the other hand, I agree with the Court that it would be anomalous for a locked compartment in an automobile to be unprotected by the "general requirement" of a prior warrant, but for an unlocked briefcase within the automobile to be protected. I join in the judgment of the Court because I think its holding is more faithful to the text and tradition of the Fourth

Amendment, and if these anomalies in our jurisprudence are ever to be eliminated that is the direction in which we should travel.

* * *

Although the Fourth Amendment does not explicitly impose the requirement of a warrant, it is of course textually possible to consider that implicit within the requirement of reasonableness. For some years after the (still continuing) explosion in Fourth Amendment litigation that followed our announcement of the exclusionary rule in Weeks v. United States, 232 U.S. 383, 34 S.Ct. 341, 58 L.Ed. 652 (1914), our jurisprudence lurched back and forth between imposing a categorical warrant requirement and looking to reasonableness alone. By the late 1960's, the preference for a warrant had won out, at least rhetorically.

The victory was illusory. Even before today's decision, the "warrant requirement" had become so riddled with exceptions that it was basically unrecognizable. * * *

Unlike the dissent, therefore, I do not regard today's holding as some momentous departure, but rather as merely the continuation of an inconsistent jurisprudence that has been with us for years. * * * There can be no clarity in this area unless we make up our minds, and unless the principles we express comport with the actions we take.

In my view, the path out of this confusion should be sought by returning to the first principle that the "reasonableness" requirement of the Fourth Amendment affords the protection that the common law afforded. I have no difficulty with the proposition that includes the requirement of a warrant, where the common law required a warrant * * *. But the supposed "general rule" that a warrant is always required does not appear to have any basis in the common law and confuses rather than facilitates any attempt to develop rules of reasonableness in light of changed legal circumstances, as the anomaly eliminated and the anomaly created by today's holding both demonstrate.

* * *

I would reverse the judgment in the present case, not because a closed container carried inside a car becomes subject to the "automobile" exception to the general warrant requirement, but because the search of a closed container, outside a privately owned building, with probable cause to believe that the container contains contraband, and when it in fact does contain contraband, is not one of those searches whose Fourth Amendment reasonableness depends upon a warrant. For that reason I concur in the judgment of the Court.

JUSTICE WHITE, dissenting.

Agreeing as I do with most of JUSTICE STEVENS' opinion and with the result he reaches, I dissent and would affirm the judgment below.

JUSTICE STEVENS, with whom JUSTICE MARSHALL joins, dissenting.

* * *

II

In its opinion today, the Court recognizes that the police did not have probable cause to search respondent's vehicle and that a search of anything but the paper bag that respondent had carried from Daza's apartment and placed in the trunk of his car would have been unconstitutional. Moreover, as I read the opinion, the Court assumes that the police could not have made a warrantless inspection of the bag before it was placed in the car. Finally, the Court also does not question the fact that, under our prior cases, it would have been lawful for the police to seize the container and detain it (and respondent) until they obtained a search warrant. Thus, all of the relevant facts that governed our decisions in *Chadwick* and *Sanders* are present here whereas the relevant fact that justified the vehicle search in *Ross* is not present.

The Court does not attempt to identify any exigent circumstances that would justify its refusal to apply the general rule against warrantless searches. Instead, it advances these three arguments: First, the rules identified in [*Chadwick* and *Sanders*] are confusing and anomalous. Second, the rules do not protect any significant interest in privacy. And, third, the rules impede effective law enforcement. None of these arguments withstands scrutiny.

The "Confusion"

* * *

The decided cases * * * provide no support for the Court's concern about "confusion." * * *

The Court summarizes the alleged "anomaly" created by the coexistence of *Ross, Chadwick,* and *Sanders* with the statement that "the more likely the police are to discover drugs in a container, the less authority they have to search it." This juxtaposition is only anomalous, however, if one accepts the flawed premise that the degree to which the police are likely to discover contraband is correlated with their authority to search without a warrant. Yet, even proof beyond a reasonable doubt will not justify a warrantless search that is not supported by one of the exceptions to the warrant requirement. And, even when the police have a warrant or an exception applies, once the police possess probable cause, the extent to which they are more or less certain of the contents of a container has no bearing on their authority to search it.

To the extent there was any "anomaly" in our prior jurisprudence, the Court has "cured" it at the expense of creating a more serious paradox. For, surely it is anomalous to prohibit a search of a briefcase while the owner is carrying it exposed on a public street yet to permit a search once the owner has placed the briefcase in the locked trunk of his car. One's privacy interest in one's luggage can certainly not be diminished by one's removing it from a public thoroughfare and placing it—out of sight—in a privately owned vehicle. Nor is the danger that evidence will escape increased if the luggage is in a car rather than on the street. In either location, if the police have probable cause, they are authorized to seize the luggage and to detain it until they obtain judicial approval for a search. Any line demarking an exception to the warrant requirement will appear blurred at the edges, but the Court has certainly erred if it believes that, by erasing one line and drawing another, it has drawn a clearer boundary.

The Privacy Argument

The Court's statement that *Chadwick* and *Sanders* provide only "minimal protection to privacy," is also unpersuasive. Every citizen clearly has an interest in the privacy of the contents of his or her luggage, briefcase, handbag or any other container that conceals private papers and effects from public scrutiny. That privacy interest has been recognized repeatedly in cases spanning more than a century.

Under the Court's holding today, the privacy interest that protects the contents of a suitcase or a briefcase from a warrantless search when it is in public view simply vanishes when its owner climbs into a taxicab. Unquestionably the rejection of the *Sanders* line of cases by today's decision will result in a significant loss of individual privacy.

* * *

The Burden on Law Enforcement

The Court's suggestion that *Chadwick* and *Sanders* have created a significant burden on effective law enforcement is unsupported, inaccurate, and, in any event, an insufficient reason for creating a new exception to the warrant requirement.

Despite repeated claims that *Chadwick* and *Sanders* have "impeded effective law enforcement," the Court cites no authority for its contentions. * * *

Even if the warrant requirement does inconvenience the police to some extent, that fact does not distinguish this constitutional requirement from any other procedural protection secured by the Bill of Rights. It is merely a part of the price that our society must pay in order to preserve its freedom. * * *

I respectfully dissent.

Chapter 7

INTERROGATION AND CONFESSIONS

A. THE REQUIREMENT OF VOLUNTARINESS

Page 413. Add the following at the end of the discussion of *Promises* in the Editors' Introduction:

The Supreme Court addressed the constitutional significance of promises in Arizona v. Fulminante, 499 U.S. 279, 111 S.Ct. 1246, 113 L.Ed.2d 302 (1991). Fulminante had been a prisoner in a federal correctional facility and had begun to receive "rough treatment" from other inmates because of a rumor that he had killed a child. Sarivola was a fellow inmate who was also an informant for the Federal Bureau of Investigation. Federal agents encouraged Sarivola to elicit information about the killing from Fulminante. Sarivola then offered to protect Fulminante from other inmates if Fulminante told him about the matter. Fulminante admitted the killing to Sarivola. At Fulminante's trial for the murder of the child, his confession was offered. The Arizona Supreme Court held that it was inadmissible. This was challenged by the State on the ground that the Arizona court had incorrectly applied a standard under which the confession was involuntary upon proof that "but for" the "promise" by Sarivola, the confession would not have been given. The Supreme Court noted the *Bram* discussion but made clear that this was no longer controlling:

> Although the Court noted in *Bram* that a confession cannot be obtained by " 'any direct or implied promises, however slight, nor by the exertion of any improper influence,' " it is clear this passage from *Bram* * * * does not state the standard for determining the voluntariness of a confession * * *.

499 U.S. at 285, 111 S.Ct. at 1251, 113 L.Ed.2d at 315. But it further found that the Arizona court had properly applied a totality of the circumstances analysis. Although the question was a "close one," the majority concluded that the Arizona court acceptably found the confession involuntary:

> The Arizona Supreme Court found a credible threat of physical violence unless Fulminante confessed. Our cases have made clear that a finding of coercion need not depend upon actual violence by a government agent; a credible threat is sufficient. * * * [T]he Arizona Supreme Court found that it was fear of physical violence, absent protection from his friend (and Government agent) Sarivola, which motivated Fulminante to confess. Accepting the Arizona

> court's finding, permissible on this record, that there was a credible threat of physical violence, we agree with its conclusion that Fulminante's will was overborne in such a way as to render his confession the product of coercion.

499 U.S. at 287, 111 S.Ct. at 1252–53, 113 L.Ed.2d at 316–17.

Page 425. Add the following new notes after Colorado v. Connelly:

2a. Under Gerstein v. Pugh, 420 U.S. 103, 95 S.Ct. 854, 43 L.Ed.2d 54 (1975), an unindicted defendant arrested without a warrant has a Fourth Amendment right to a "prompt" judicial determination of probable cause. Under County of Riverside v. McLaughlin, 500 U.S. 44, 111 S.Ct. 1661, 114 L.Ed.2d 49 (1991), promptness generally requires that such probable cause determinations be made within 48 hours of arrests. These determinations may—but need not—be made when the defendants are presented before magistrates pursuant to the statutory provisions discussed in note 2, above. If an arrested defendant is detained without compliance with this right and after the detention has become violative of this right the defendant makes a confession, does the Fourth Amendment require exclusion of the confession?

The issue was noted but not addressed by the Supreme Court in Powell v. Nevada, ___ U.S. ___, ___, 114 S.Ct. 1280, 1283–84, 128 L.Ed.2d 1, 7–8 (1994). Justice Thomas, joined by the Chief Justice, argued in *Powell* that the Court should reach the issue. He further offered an analysis that would render suppression inappropriate in some and perhaps all such cases. Powell had been arrested on November 3, 1989 after he brought a badly injured child to a hospital for treatment. On November 7, he made a statement admitting abusing the child. Later on the 7th, a magistrate determined that the arrest had been supported by probable cause; the magistrate relied upon facts recited in a "declaration of arrest" prepared by officers within an hour of Powell's arrest. On these facts, Justice Thomas reasoned, the November 7th statement need not be suppressed:

> [S]uppression of petitioner's statement would not be appropriate because the statement was not a product of the *McLaughlin* violation.
>
> Our decisions make clear "that evidence will not be excluded as 'fruit' [of an unlawful act] unless the illegality is at least the 'but for' cause of the discovery of the evidence." * * *
>
> Contrary to petitioner's arguments, the violation of *McLaughlin* (as opposed to his arrest and custody) bore no causal relationship whatsoever to his November 7 statement. The timing of the probable cause determination would have affected petitioner's statement only if a proper hearing at or before the 48–hour mark would have resulted in a finding of no probable cause. Yet, as the magistrate found, the police had probable cause to suspect petitioner of child abuse, and there is no suggestion that the delay in securing a determination of probable cause permitted the police to gather additional evidence to be presented to the magistrate. On the contrary, the magistrate based his determination on the facts included in the declaration of arrest that was completed within an hour of petitioner's arrest. Thus, if the probable cause determination had been made within 48 hours as required by *McLaughlin,* the same information would have been presented,

the same result would have been obtained, and none of the circumstances of petitioner's custody would have been altered.

Moreover, it cannot be argued that the *McLaughlin* error somehow made petitioner's custody unlawful and thereby rendered the statement the product of unlawful custody. Because the arresting officers had probable cause to arrest petitioner, he was lawfully arrested at the hospital. Cf. [New York v.] Harris, [495 U.S. 14, 18, 110 S.Ct. 1640, 1643, 109 L.Ed.2d 13 (1990)]. The presumptively unconstitutional delay in securing a judicial determination of probable cause during a period of lawful custody did not render that custody illegal. We have never suggested that lawful custody becomes unlawful due to a failure to obtain a prompt judicial finding of probable cause—that is, probable cause does not disappear if not judicially determined within 48 hours.

___ U.S. at ___ 114 S.Ct. at 1286–87, 128 L.Ed.2d at 10–12 (Thomas, J., dissenting). Since the confession was not the product of illegal governmental activity, he added, "conventional attenuation principles are inapplicable in this case * * *." ___ U.S. at ___ n. 2, 114 S.Ct. at 1287 n. 2, 128 L.Ed.2d at 12 n. 2.

2b. Earlier Supreme Court discussions had suggested that if on appeal an appellate court determined that the trial judge had erroneously admitted an involuntary confession, reversal of the conviction for a new trial of the defendant was always necessary. In Arizona v. Fulminante, 499 U.S. 279, 111 S.Ct. 1246, 113 L.Ed.2d 302 (1991), however, a bare majority of the Supreme Court held that even admission of an involuntary confession could be harmless error if the appellate court is convinced beyond a reasonable doubt that the confession did not contribute to the defendant's conviction. Trial errors generally are subject to the harmless error rule, the court concluded, and insufficient reason exists to treat involuntary confessions any differently. Admission of such a confession is not a "structural defect[ ] in the constitution of the trial mechanism, which def[ies] analysis by 'harmless error' standards." Nor is the admission of such a confession a type of error that should always require reversal because it "transcends the criminal process." 499 U.S. at 306–12, 111 S.Ct. at 1263–66, 113 L.Ed.2d at 329–33. On the facts of *Fulminante,* however, the State failed to meet its burden of establishing beyond a reasonable doubt that the confession did not contribute to Fulminante's conviction. Therefore, the conviction had to be reversed. 499 U.S. at 295–302, 111 S.Ct. at 1257–61, 113 L.Ed.2d at 322–26.

B. SELF-INCRIMINATION AND MIRANDA'S RIGHT TO COUNSEL

1. THE *MIRANDA* DECISION

Page 444. Insert the following additional note between notes 3 and 4 after Miranda v. Arizona:

3a. In Stone v. Powell, 428 U.S. 465, 96 S.Ct. 3037, 49 L.Ed.2d 1067 (1976), discussed in the note on page 25 of the text, the Supreme Court held that a person convicted in state court was not entitled to federal habeas corpus relief on the ground that evidence obtained in violation of the Fourth Amendment had been used in his trial in violation of Mapp v. Ohio, 367 U.S. 643, 81 S.Ct. 1684, 6 L.Ed.2d 1081 (1961), if the state courts had provided him with an opportunity for full and fair litigation of his Fourth Amendment claim. Whether a person convicted in state court is similarly limited in obtaining federal habeas corpus relief on the ground that evidence obtained in violation of *Miranda* was used at his trial was finally considered in Withrow v. Williams, ___ U.S. ___, 113 S.Ct. 1745, 123 L.Ed.2d 407 (1993). By a 5–to–4 vote, the Court held that it would not take the *Stone* approach when a state defendant sought federal habeas corpus on *Miranda* grounds. The Michigan state courts in which petitioner Pamela Withrow had been convicted had given her a full and fair opportunity to litigate her claim that *Miranda* demanded exclusion of her confession. Nevertheless, the lower federal courts acted properly in holding that conviction invalid because the Michigan courts mistakenly determined that her confession was admissible despite *Miranda*.

The reasons for not applying *Stone's* approach to *Miranda* claims, Justice Souter explained for the majority, rest in part upon differences between *Mapp* and *Miranda*. *Mapp* created no personal constitutional right; *Miranda's* requirements, in contrast, safeguard defendants' Fifth Amendment privilege against self-incrimination, "a fundamental *trial* right." *Mapp* protects privacy rights divorced from the correct ascertainment of guilt in criminal trials. *Miranda,* on the other hand "serves to guard against 'the use of unreliable statements at trial' " "[b]y bracing against 'the possibility of unreliable statements in every instance of in-custody interrogation[.]' "

Most importantly, Justice Souter continued, state prisoners barred from raising *Miranda* claims in federal habeas corpus would simply convert those claims into due process claims that involuntary confessions had been used. Federal courts' workload would not be lightened by limiting habeas petitioners' ability to raise *Miranda* claims; federal judges would simply be confronted with due process involuntariness rather than *Miranda* claims. Nor would this change in the form of claims made by state prisoners go far towards reducing tensions between the state and federal judicial systems. "[E]liminating review of *Miranda* claims," Justice Souter concluded, "would not significantly benefit the federal courts in their exercise of habeas jurisdiction, or advance the cause of federalism in any substantial way." ___ U.S. at ___, 113 S.Ct. at 1754, 123 L.Ed.2d at 420.

Justice O'Connor disagreed:

> When [a] case is on direct review, [the] damage [done by *Miranda*] to the truth-seeking function is deemed an acceptable sacrifice for the deterrence and respect for constitutional values that the *Miranda* rule brings. But once a case is on collateral review, the balance between the costs and benefits shifts; the interests of federalism, finality, and fairness compel *Miranda's* exclusion from habeas. The benefit of enforcing *Miranda* through habeas is marginal at best. To the extent *Miranda* ensures the exclusion of involuntary statements, that task can be performed more accurately by adjudicating the voluntariness question directly. And, to the extent exclusion of voluntary but unwarned confessions serves a deterrent function, "[t]he awarding of habeas relief years after conviction will often strike like lightning, and it is absurd to think that this added possibility * * * will have any appreciable effect on police training or behavior." * * *
>
> Despite its meager benefits, the relitigation of *Miranda* claims on habeas imposes substantial costs. Just like the application of the exclusion-

> ary rule, application of *Miranda's* prophylactic rule on habeas consumes scarce judicial resources on an issue unrelated to guilt or innocence. No less than the exclusionary rule, it undercuts finality. It creates tension between the state and federal courts. And it upsets the division of responsibilities that underlies our federal system. But most troubling of all, *Miranda's* application on habeas sometimes precludes the just application of law altogether. The order excluding the statement will often be issued "years after trial, when a new trial may be a practical impossibility." Whether the Court admits it or not, the grim result of applying *Miranda* on habeas will be, time and time again, "the release of an admittedly guilty individual who may pose a continuing threat to society."

___ U.S. at ___, 113 S.Ct. at 1759–60, 123 L.Ed.2d at 427–28 (O'Connor, J., concurring and dissenting). "In light of the meager deterrent benefit it brings and the tremendous costs it imposes," Justice O'Connor continued, "in my view application of *Miranda's* prophylactic rule on habeas 'falls short' of justification." The Chief Justice joined Justice O'Connor's opinion. Justice Scalia, joined by Justice Thomas, also dissented from the majority's failure to apply *Stone's* approach to *Miranda* claims.

2. APPLICABILITY OF *MIRANDA*

---

b. The Requirement of "Custody"

Page 460. Add the following to the introductory note by inserting it after the quotation from *Murphy:*

In 1994, the Court returned to the custody problem in Stansbury v. California, ___ U.S. ___, 114 S.Ct. 1526, 128 L.Ed.2d 293 (1994) (per curiam). Officers investigating the rape and murder of a ten year old girl learned that on the day of her death the victim had been seen talking to Stansbury, an ice cream truck driver. At 11:00 p.m., four officers went to Stansbury's trailer home and asked if he would accompany them to the police station to answer some questions. He agreed. During the subsequent questioning conducted without *Miranda* warnings, he made incriminating admissions. The state court held the statement nevertheless admissible, stressing in part that suspicion had not focused on Stansbury until he made the statement. The Supreme Court responded:

> Our decisions make clear that the initial determination of custody depends on the objective circumstances of the interrogation, not on the subjective views harbored by either the interrogating officers or the person being questioned. * * *
>
> * * * [A] police officer's subjective view that the individual under questioning is a suspect, if undisclosed, does not bear upon the question whether the individual is in custody for purposes of *Miranda.* The same principle obtains if an officer's undisclosed assessment is that the person being questioned is not a suspect. In either instance, one cannot expect the person under interrogation to probe the officer's innermost thoughts. Save as they are communicated or otherwise manifested to the person being questioned, an officer's evolving but unarticulated suspicions do not affect

> the objective circumstances of an interrogation or interview, and thus cannot affect the *Miranda* custody inquiry. * * *
>
> An officer's knowledge or beliefs may bear upon the custody issue if they are conveyed, by word or deed, to the individual being questioned. Those beliefs are relevant only to the extent they would affect how a reasonable person in the position of the individual being questioned would gauge the breadth of his or her " 'freedom of action.' " Even a clear statement from an officer that the person under interrogation is a prime suspect is not, in itself, dispositive of the custody issue, for some suspects are free to come and go until the police decide to make an arrest. The weight and pertinence of any communications regarding the officer's degree of suspicion will depend upon the facts and circumstances of the particular case. In sum, an officer's views concerning the nature of an interrogation, or beliefs concerning the potential culpability of the individual being questioned, may be one among many factors that bear upon the assessment whether that individual was in custody, but only if the officer's views or beliefs were somehow manifested to the individual under interrogation and would have affected how a reasonable person in that position would perceive his or her freedom to leave. (Of course, instances may arise in which the officer's undisclosed views are relevant in testing the credibility of his or her account of what happened during an interrogation; but it is the objective surroundings, and not any undisclosed views, that control the *Miranda* custody inquiry.)

___ U.S. at ___, 114 S.Ct. at 1529–30, 128 L.Ed.2d at 298–300. The state court's analysis suggested that the court may have regarded the officers' subjective beliefs regarding Stansbury's status "as significant in and of themselves, rather than as relevant only to the extent they influenced the objective conditions surrounding his interrogation." Nevertheless, the parties disagreed on whether the objective facts in the record supported a finding that Stansbury was in custody. Concluding that the state court should consider this question in the first instance, the Supreme Court reversed the judgment of the state tribunal and remanded the case "for further proceedings not inconsistent with this opinion." ___ U.S. at ___, 114 S.Ct. at 1531, 128 L.Ed.2d at 301.

On remand, the California Supreme Court held that under the analysis directed by the Supreme Court's opinion, the record supported the trial court's finding that Stansbury was not in custody. "[T]he record indicates," the state court concluded, "that a reasonable person in defendant's shoes would not consider that he or she was in custody." It stressed that the officers informed Stansbury that he was a possible witness and asked him to come to the station. They invited him to sit in the front seat of their vehicle. Further:

> the nature of the interview in this case, which was brief and not accusatory, would not convey to the reasonable person the impression that he or she was in custody, despite the fact that the interview took place in an interview room in the jail area of the police station.

People v. Stansbury, 9 Cal.4th 824, 832, 889 P.2d 588, 592, 38 Cal.Rptr.2d 394, 398 (1995).

3. WAIVER OF THE MIRANDA RIGHTS

Page 489. Insert the following additional note between notes 1 and 2 after Edwards v. Arizona:

1a. In Minnick v. Mississippi, 498 U.S. 146, 111 S.Ct. 486, 112 L.Ed.2d 489 (1990), Minnick was interviewed by FBI agents and told them, "Come back Monday when I have a lawyer." The federal officers ended the interview. Minnick later met with a lawyer appointed to represent him and spoke with that attorney—perhaps by telephone—on several other occasions. A state officer then interviewed Minnick after warning him of his *Miranda* rights; Minnick refused to sign a waiver form but talked with the officer and made incriminating admissions. The state court declined to apply *Edwards,* reasoning that in *Edwards* itself the Supreme Court indicated that the bar to further interrogation applies only "until counsel has been made available to [the suspect]," and the consultations between Minnick and his lawyer established that counsel had been "made available." The Supreme Court reversed, concluding that *Edwards* applied, the police-initiated interrogation by the state officer was impermissible, and Minnick's statement to him was thus inadmissible. Justice Kennedy explained for the Court:

> [W]e * * * hold that when counsel is requested, interrogation must cease, and officials may not reinstate interrogation without counsel present, whether or not the accused has consulted with his attorney.
>
> We consider our ruling to be an appropriate and necessary application of the *Edwards* rule. A single consultation with an attorney does not remove the suspect from persistent attempts by officials to persuade him to waive his right, or from the coercive pressures that accompany custody and that may increase as custody is prolonged. * * *
>
> The exception proposed * * * would undermine the advantages flowing from *Edwards'* "clear and unequivocal" character. * * * [It] would leave far from certain the sort of consultation required to displace *Edwards.* * * *
>
> [We are also concerned] that the suspect whose counsel is prompt would lose the protection of *Edwards,* while the one whose counsel is dilatory would not. There is more than irony in this rule. There is a strong possibility that it would distort the proper concept of the attorney's duty to the client and set us on a course at odds with what ought to be effective representation.
>
> * * *

498 U.S. at 153–55, 111 S.Ct. at 491–92, 112 L.Ed.2d at 498–99.

Justice Scalia, joined by the Chief Justice, dissented, arguing that *Edwards* should cease to apply after the initial consultation between the suspect and his attorney:

> The suspect then knows he had an advocate on his side, and that the police will permit him to consult that advocate. He almost certainly also has a heightened awareness (above what the *Miranda* warning itself will provide) of his right to remain silent * * *.

498 U.S. at 162, 111 S.Ct. at 496, 112 L.Ed.2d at 503 (Scalia, J., dissenting). He stressed the extent to which the majority's holding will constrict law enforcement:

> Today's ruling that the invocation of a right to counsel permanently prevents a police-initiated waiver, makes it largely impossible for the police to urge a prisoner who has initially declined to confess to change his mind—or indeed, even to ask whether he has changed his mind. Many persons in custody will invoke the *Miranda* right to counsel during the first interrogation, so that the permanent prohibition will attach at once. Those who do not do so will almost certainly request or obtain counsel at arraignment. * * *

498 U.S. at 163, 111 S.Ct. at 496, 112 L.Ed.2d at 504. Turning to more general considerations, he continued:

> [E]ven in *Edwards* itself, but surely in today's decision, we have gone far beyond any genuine concern about suspects who do not *know* their right to remain silent, or who have been *coerced* to abandon it. Both holdings are explicable, in my view, only as an effort to protect suspects against what is regarded as their own folly. * * * Apart from the fact that this protective enterprise is beyond our authority under the Fifth Amendment or any other provision of the Constitution, it is unwise. * * *
>
> [E]ven if I were to concede that an honest confession is a foolish mistake, I would welcome rather than reject it; a rule that foolish mistakes do not count would leave most offenders not only unconvicted but undetected. More fundamentally, however, it is wrong, and subtly corrosive of our criminal justice system, to regard an honest confession as a "mistake." While every person is entitled to remain silent, it is more virtuous for the wrongdoer to admit his offense and accept the punishment he deserves. Not only for society, but for the wrongdoer himself, "admissio[n] of guilt * * *, if not coerced, [is] inherently desirable," because it advances the goals of both "justice *and* rehabilitation." * * * We should, then, rejoice at the "poor fool" who has made [an honest confession]; and we should regret the attempted retraction of that good act, rather than seek to facilitate and encourage it. To design our laws on premises contrary to these is to abandon belief in either personal responsibility or the moral claim of just government to obedience. * * *

498 U.S. at 166–67, 111 S.Ct. at 497–98, 112 L.Ed.2d at 506.

Page 491. Add the following to note 3 after Edwards v. Arizona:

The Court finally addressed suspects' ambiguous references to counsel in Davis v. United States, ___ U.S. ___, 114 S.Ct. 2350, 129 L.Ed.2d 362 (1994). Petitioner Davis, while in custody, was interviewed by agents of the Naval Investigative Service (NIS) concerning a homicide. The Court described the events as follows:

> About an hour and a half into the interview, petitioner said, "Maybe I should talk to a lawyer." According to the uncontradicted testimony of one of the interviewing agents, the interview then proceeded as follows: "[We m]ade it very clear that we're not here to violate his rights, that if he wants a lawyer, then we will stop any kind of questioning with him, that we

> weren't going to pursue the matter unless we have it clarified is he asking for a lawyer or is he just making a comment about a lawyer, and he said, [']No, I'm not asking for a lawyer,' and then he continued on, and said, 'No, I don't want a lawyer.' " After a short break, the agents reminded petitioner of his rights to remain silent and to counsel. The interview then continued for another hour, until petitioner said, "I think I want a lawyer before I say anything else." At that point, questioning ceased.

At Davis' general court-martial, his statements during the questioning were admitted and the United States Court of Military Appeals affirmed. It held that Davis' remark—"Maybe I should talk to a lawyer"—was not a request for counsel. Under *Miranda,* it continued, when a suspect ambiguously mentions counsel as Davis did but does not request representation, all interrogation about the offense must cease. The interrogators may, however, ask narrow questions designed to clarify his remark and his desire for counsel. The agents here, the court concluded, complied with this requirement.

The Supreme Court affirmed but indicated that the Court of Military Appeals had gone further than necessary:

> The applicability of the " 'rigid' prophylactic rule" of *Edwards* requires courts to "determine whether the accused actually invoked his right to counsel." To avoid difficulties of proof and to provide guidance to officers conducting interrogations, this is an objective inquiry. Invocation of the *Miranda* right to counsel "requires, at a minimum, some statement that can reasonably be construed to be an expression of a desire for the assistance of an attorney." But if a suspect makes a reference to an attorney that is ambiguous or equivocal in that a reasonable officer in light of the circumstances would have understood only that the suspect might be invoking the right to counsel, our precedents do not require the cessation of questioning.
>
> Rather, the suspect must unambiguously request counsel. As we have observed, "a statement either is such an assertion of the right to counsel or it is not." Smith v. Illinois, 469 U.S., at 97–98 (brackets and internal quotation marks omitted). Although a suspect need not "speak with the discrimination of an Oxford don," he must articulate his desire to have counsel present sufficiently clearly that a reasonable police officer in the circumstances would understand the statement to be a request for an attorney. If the statement fails to meet the requisite level of clarity, *Edwards* does not require that the officers stop questioning the suspect.
>
> We decline petitioner's invitation to extend *Edwards* and require law enforcement officers to cease questioning immediately upon the making of an ambiguous or equivocal reference to an attorney. The rationale underlying *Edwards* is that the police must respect a suspect's wishes regarding his right to have an attorney present during custodial interrogation. But when the officers conducting the questioning reasonably do not know whether or not the suspect wants a lawyer, a rule requiring the immediate cessation of questioning "would transform the *Miranda* safeguards into wholly irrational obstacles to legitimate police investigative activity," because it would needlessly prevent the police from questioning a suspect in the absence of counsel even if the suspect did not wish to have a lawyer present. Nothing in *Edwards* requires the provision of counsel to a suspect who consents to answer questions without the assistance of a lawyer. * * *

> We recognize that requiring a clear assertion of the right to counsel might disadvantage some suspects who—because of fear, intimidation, lack of linguistic skills, or a variety of other reasons—will not clearly articulate their right to counsel although they actually want to have a lawyer present. But the primary protection afforded suspects subject to custodial interrogation is the *Miranda* warnings themselves. "[F]ull comprehension of the rights to remain silent and request an attorney [is] sufficient to dispel whatever coercion is inherent in the interrogation process." A suspect who knowingly and voluntarily waives his right to counsel after having that right explained to him has indicated his willingness to deal with the police unassisted. Although *Edwards* provides an additional protection—if a suspect subsequently requests an attorney, questioning must cease—it is one that must be affirmatively invoked by the suspect.
>
> In considering how a suspect must invoke the right to counsel, we must consider the other side of the *Miranda* equation: the need for effective law enforcement. Although the courts ensure compliance with the *Miranda* requirements through the exclusionary rule, it is police officers who must actually decide whether or not they can question a suspect. The *Edwards* rule—questioning must cease if the suspect asks for a lawyer—provides a bright line that can be applied by officers in the real world of investigation and interrogation without unduly hampering the gathering of information. But if we were to require questioning to cease if a suspect makes a statement that might be a request for an attorney, this clarity and ease of application would be lost. Police officers would be forced to make difficult judgment calls about whether the suspect in fact wants a lawyer even though he hasn't said so, with the threat of suppression if they guess wrong. We therefore hold that, after a knowing and voluntary waiver of the *Miranda* rights, law enforcement officers may continue questioning until and unless the suspect clearly requests an attorney.
>
> Of course, when a suspect makes an ambiguous or equivocal statement it will often be good police practice for the interviewing officers to clarify whether or not he actually wants an attorney. That was the procedure followed by the NIS agents in this case. Clarifying questions help protect the rights of the suspect by ensuring that he gets an attorney if he wants one, and will minimize the chance of a confession being suppressed due to subsequent judicial second-guessing as to the meaning of the suspect's statement regarding counsel. But we decline to adopt a rule requiring officers to ask clarifying questions. If the suspect's statement is not an unambiguous or unequivocal request for counsel, the officers have no obligation to stop questioning him.

___ U.S. at ___, 114 S.Ct. at 2355–56, 129 L.Ed.2d at 371–73. The courts below had held that Davis' reference to a lawyer was not a request for counsel and the Supreme Court declined to disturb that conclusion. Therefore, the NIS agents had not been required to cease their questioning of Davis because of that reference and their continued questioning of him provided no basis for suppressing his statements.

Justice Souter, joined by Justices Blackmun, Stevens and Ginsburg, concurred in the judgment. He agreed with the majority's rejection of Davis' argument that even ambiguous references to counsel should require an end to all police questioning. But in contrast with the majority, he argued:

> Our cases are best respected by a rule that when a suspect under custodial interrogation makes an ambiguous statement that might reasonably be understood as expressing a wish that a lawyer be summoned (and questioning cease), interrogators' questions should be confined to verifying whether the individual meant to ask for a lawyer.

___ U.S., at ___, 114 S.Ct., at 2364, 129 L.Ed.2d at 382 (Souter, J., concurring in the judgment). He explained:

> Throughout [our three decades of *Miranda* case law], two precepts have commanded broad assent: that the *Miranda* safeguards exist "to assure that the individual's right to choose between speech and silence remains unfettered throughout the interrogation process," and that the justification for *Miranda* rules, intended to operate in the real world, "must be consistent with * * * practical realities." A rule barring government agents from further interrogation until they determine whether a suspect's ambiguous statement was meant as a request for counsel fulfills both ambitions. It assures that a suspect's choice whether or not to deal with police through counsel will be "scrupulously honored," and it faces both the real-world reasons why misunderstandings arise between suspect and interrogator and the real-world limitations on the capacity of police and trial courts to apply fine distinctions and intricate rules.
>
> * * *
>
> Tested against the same two principles, the approach the Court adopts does not fare so well. First, as the majority expressly acknowledges, criminal suspects who may (in *Miranda's* words) be "thrust into an unfamiliar atmosphere and run through menacing police interrogation procedures," would seem an odd group to single out for the Court's demand of heightened linguistic care. A substantial percentage of them lack anything like a confident command of the English language, and many more will be sufficiently intimidated by the interrogation process or overwhelmed by the uncertainty of their predicament that the ability to speak assertively will abandon them. * * *
>
> Nor may the standard governing waivers as expressed in these statements be deflected away by drawing a distinction between initial waivers of *Miranda* rights and subsequent decisions to reinvoke them, on the theory that so long as the burden to demonstrate waiver rests on the government, it is only fair to make the suspect shoulder a burden of showing a clear subsequent assertion. *Miranda* itself discredited the legitimacy of any such distinction. The opinion described the object of the warning as being to assure "a continuous opportunity to exercise [the right of silence]." "[C]ontinuous opportunity" suggests an unvarying one, governed by a common standard of effectiveness. * * *
>
> The Court defends as tolerable the certainty that some poorly expressed requests for counsel will be disregarded on the ground that *Miranda* warnings suffice to alleviate the inherent coercion of the custodial interrogation. But, "a once-stated warning, delivered by those who will conduct the interrogation cannot itself suffice" to "assure that the ... right to choose

between silence and speech remains unfettered throughout the interrogation process." * * *

Indeed, it is easy, amidst the discussion of layers of protection, to lose sight of a real risk in the majority's approach, going close to the core of what the Court has held that the Fifth Amendment provides. * * * When a suspect understands his (expressed) wishes to have been ignored (and by hypothesis, he has said something that an objective listener could "reasonably," although not necessarily, take to be a request), in contravention of the "rights" just read to him by his interrogator, he may well see further objection as futile and confession (true or not) as the only way to end his interrogation. Nor is it enough to say that a " 'statement either is * * * an assertion of the right to counsel or it is not." ' * * * While it might be fair to say that every statement is meant either to express a desire to deal with police through counsel or not, this fact does not dictate the rule that interrogators who hear a statement consistent with either possibility may presume the latter and forge ahead; on the contrary, clarification is the intuitively sensible course.

The other justifications offered for the "requisite level of clarity" rule, are that, whatever its costs, it will further society's strong interest in "effective law enforcement," and maintain the "ease of application" that has long been a concern of our *Miranda* jurisprudence. With respect to the first point, the margin of difference between the clarification approach advocated here and the one the Court adopts is defined by the class of cases in which a suspect, if asked, would make it plain that he meant to request counsel (at which point questioning would cease). While these lost confessions do extract a real price from society, it is one that *Miranda* itself determined should be borne.

As for practical application, while every approach, including the majority's, will involve some "difficult judgment calls," the rule argued for here would relieve the officer of any responsibility for guessing "whether the suspect in fact wants a lawyer even though he hasn't said so." To the contrary, it would assure that the "judgment call" will be made by the party most competent to resolve the ambiguity, who our case law has always assumed should make it: the individual suspect.

* * *

* * * While there is reason to expect that trial courts will apply today's ruling sensibly (without requiring criminal suspects to speak with the discrimination of an Oxford don) and that interrogators will continue to follow what the Court rightly calls "good police practice" (compelled up to now by a substantial body of state and Circuit law), I believe that the case law under *Miranda* does not allow them to do otherwise.

___ U.S. at ___, 114 S.Ct. at 2360–64, 129 L.Ed.2d at 377–82.

Page 491. Add the following new notes after Edwards v. Arizona:

1b. The limits of *Edwards' per se* approach were presented to the Supreme Court in United States v. Green, 592 A.2d 985 (D.C.App.1991), cert. granted 504 U.S. 908, 112 S.Ct. 1935, 18 L.Ed.2d 542 (1992). Green had been arrested on July 19, 1989 for possession of a controlled substance. When presented with a printed form inquiring whether he was willing to talk with the police without an attorney being present, he wrote in, "No." Green remained in jail. On September 27, he pled guilty to a lesser included offense and was transferred to a juvenile facility while a presentence report was being prepared. On January 4, 1990, an arrest warrant was issued for him in connection with an unrelated murder charge. On January 5, he was transported to the police Homicide Office for processing on the murder charge. Officers warned him of his *Miranda* rights, he waived those rights, and he made a videotaped confession to the murder. On February 26, 1990, he was sentenced to fifteen months for the drug charge.

Before his murder trial, he moved to suppress his confession, arguing that the police action on January 5, 1990 constituted interrogation in violation of *Edwards.* The trial judge refused to suppress the conviction. Then the Supreme Court decided Minnick v. Mississippi, 498 U.S. 146, 111 S.Ct. 486, 112 L.Ed.2d 489 (1990), discussed in the preceding note. The trial judge reconsidered his ruling in light of *Minnick* and decided that suppression was required in light of *Minnick's* holding that consultation with counsel did not render *Edwards* inapplicable and the opinion's emphasis upon the "bright line" nature of the *Edwards* holding. Upon the Government's appeal, the District of Columbia Court of Appeals (by a split 2–1 vote) affirmed:

> Until the Court provides further guidance, we are persuaded that so long as the defendant remains in custody, the fact that the police did not reinitiate interrogation until five months after he invoked his right to counsel cannot be adequate reason, alone or combined with the [other] factors [present in the case], to justify a departure from *Edwards'* command.

592 A.2d at 989–90. The Supreme Court granted certiorari.

In its presentation to the Supreme Court, the Government characterized *Edwards* as creating "an irrebuttable presumption of coercion" when it applies. Such a presumption should be applied, the Government argued, only where the risk of actual coercion is so great as to make such a presumption appropriate. That is not the case in situations like *Green.*

The Government stressed to the Court that three factors distinguished *Green* from other cases: the intervention of the suspect's plea of guilty to the offense between his invocation of the right to counsel and the police interrogation; the five months that intervened; and that Green was reapproached only after his initial request for counsel had been honored by providing him with counsel.

> Taken singly or in conjunction, those factors indicate that it is highly unlikely that the reinitiation of police questioning wore down [Green] and induced him to confess. For that reason, there is no justification for applying the irrebuttable presumption of the *Edwards* rule.

United States v. Green, Brief for the United States. With regard to the appropriate approach, the Government explained:

> We * * * disagree with the [court of appeal's] implicit conclusion that the *Edwards* presumption can be rebutted only by an event that conclusively established that a suspect has decided to speak with the police in counsel's absence.

> The fallacy of that position is demonstrated by the generally accepted principle that the *Edwards* presumption does not survive a break in custody. A break in custody * * * does not establish that the suspect now wishes to speak to the police directly. * * * The reason a break in custody ends the *Edwards* presumption * * * is not because it conclusively establishes that a suspect will thereafter wish to speak to the police, but rather because it is so dramatic a change in circumstances that it is no longer reasonable irrebuttably to presume the contrary.
>
> The "break in custody" cases are mere specific examples of a broader point: the irrebuttable presumption from *Edwards* should not apply when there is a significant change in the accused's status prior to the interrogation. * * * In a case such as this one, the relevant question is * * * not whether [the intervening events] conclusively establish[ ] that a suspect wishes to speak to the police directly, but whether [the events] render[ ] unreasonable the continued application of *Edwards'* irrebuttable presumption that a subsequent decision to speak with the police on their request is the product of coercion, rather than a knowing, intelligent, and voluntary decision by the suspect.

Green argued in response that none of the factors relied upon by the Government justified regarding *Edwards* as inapplicable. He particularly stressed his perception that the passage of time should not have this effect:

> The five month period of incarceration increased the pressures on [Green] by making him more vulnerable to the coercion that can accompany custodial interrogation. An additional problem associated with incarceration is the tendency of the inmate to become institutionalized to the point where he responds affirmatively to all instructions of the authorities. Finally, any change in the "bright-line rule" that would make it dependent on the length of time between the request for counsel and the reinitiation of questioning would dim or eliminate the "bright-line rule."

Brief for the Respondent. Briefs amici curiae were filed by Americans for Effective Law Enforcement, the District of Columbia, and the Public Defender Service for the District of Columbia and the National Legal Aid and Defenders Association. The Supreme Court heard oral argument in the case on December 30, 1992.

On March 26, 1993 the Washington Post reported two District of Columbia killings the prior day. At 5:15 p.m., it noted, Lowell Michael Green, age 21, had been shot several times at 18th and H Streets N.E., and died at D.C. General Hospital. Three days later, on March 29, the United States filed a memorandum with the Supreme Court suggesting that *Green* was moot because respondent Green had died. On April 5, the Court entered a per curiam order vacating the order granting certiorari and dismissing the petition for certiorari. ___ U.S. ___, 113 S.Ct. 1835, 123 L.Ed.2d 260 (1993) (per curiam).

4. The Supreme Court has held that a suspect has a Sixth Amendment right to counsel that applies—among other times—during police interrogation. This right is invoked, the Court has assumed, if a suspect appears in court with counsel representing him. The Sixth Amendment right, unlike the *Miranda–Edwards* right as construed in *Roberson,* is "offense-specific," which means it only bars officers from approaching the suspect concerning the same offense.

These holdings are considered in detail in part C of Chapter 5 on pages 523–36 of the text.

Action by a defendant that is sufficient to invoke the Sixth Amendment right to counsel, however, does not necessarily invoke the *Edwards* rule under *Miranda* and the Fifth Amendment. In McNeil v. Wisconsin, 501 U.S. 171, 111 S.Ct. 2204, 115 L.Ed.2d 158 (1991), the defendant was arrested for robbery and appeared before a court commissioner who set bail on the robbery charge. He was represented by a public defender at that appearance. A detective later approached him concerning an unrelated burglary and murder. McNeil was warned of his *Miranda* rights and waived them; he then gave a statement incriminating himself in those offenses. The Supreme Court "accepted" that McNeil's appearance before the commissioner with an attorney invoked his Sixth Amendment right to counsel with regard to the robbery. But it held that this action did not invoke McNeil's *Miranda* right to counsel so as to trigger the *Edwards* rule. Justice Scalia explained for the Court:

> [*Edwards*] requires, at a minimum, some statement that can reasonably be construed to be an expression of a desire for the assistance of an attorney *in dealing with custodial interrogation by the police.*

501 U.S. at 178, 111 S.Ct. at 2209, 115 L.Ed.2d at 169 (emphasis in original). Invoking the Sixth Amendment right to counsel concerning an offense for which one has been judicially charged does not suffice. Specifically, and with reference to the facts of *McNeil,* the Court explained, "[r]equesting the assistance of an attorney at a bail hearing does not bear that construction."

The *McNeil* Court also rejected a rule that invoking the Sixth Amendment right to counsel automatically gives the suspect the protection of *Edwards.* Such a rule would impede law enforcement objectives, it reasoned, since suspects are often offered and given counsel in their first formal court appearance.

> Thus * * * most persons in pretrial custody for serious offenses would be *unapproachable* by police officers suspecting them of involvement in other crimes, *even though they have never expressed any unwillingness to be questioned.*

501 U.S. at 179, 111 S.Ct. at 2210, 115 L.Ed.2d at 170 (emphasis in original). The rule would provide only insignificant protection for suspects:

> If a suspect does not wish to communicate with the police except through an attorney, he can simply tell them that when they give him the *Miranda* warnings. There is not the remotest chance that he will feel "badgered" by their asking to talk to him without counsel present, since the subject will not be the charge on which he has already requested counsel's assistance * * * and he will not have rejected uncounseled interrogation on *any* subject before (for in that event *Edwards* would preclude initiation of the interview).

501 U.S. at 180, 111 S.Ct. at 2210, 115 L.Ed.2d at 170.

The *McNeil* dissenters suggested that the majority's distinction will be nullified by lawyers who, on behalf of their clients, will routinely and at the first court appearance announce that their clients are invoking their *Miranda* rights. Responding, Justice Scalia questioned whether these and other "anticipatory" invocations of *Miranda* rights would be effective:

> We have * * * never held that a person can invoke his *Miranda* rights anticipatorily, in a context other than "custodial interrogation"—which a preliminary hearing will not always, or even usually, involve. If the *Miranda* right to counsel can be invoked at a preliminary hearing, it could be argued, there is no logical reason why it could not be invoked by a letter prior to arrest, or indeed even prior to identification as a suspect. Most rights must be asserted when the government seeks to take the action they protect against. The fact that we have allowed the *Miranda* right to counsel, once asserted, to be effective with respect to future custodial interrogation does not necessarily mean that we will allow it to be asserted initially outside the context of custodial interrogation, with similar future effect.

501 U.S. at 182 n. 3, 111 S.Ct. at 2211 n. 3, 115 L.Ed.2d at 171 n. 3.

Page 505. Add the following to note 3 after Moran v. Burbine:

In Minnick v. Mississippi, 498 U.S. 146, 111 S.Ct. 486, 112 L.Ed.2d 489 (1990), discussed in the material supplementing page 489 of the text, Minnick—after being warned under *Miranda*—refused to sign a "rights waiver" form but talked with an officer and made incriminating admissions. Justice Kennedy noted:

> One plausible interpretation of the record is that [Minnick] thought he could keep his admissions out of evidence by refusing to sign a formal waiver of rights.

498 U.S. at 153, 111 S.Ct. at 491, 112 L.Ed.2d at 498. The Court did not reach the effectiveness of his waiver, because it found that the officer's approach to Minnick violated the *Edwards* rule and thus required exclusion of the statement. If the Court had reached the validity of Minnick's waiver and had read the record as Justice Kennedy indicated was "plausible," would the Court have held the waiver ineffective?

Page 507. Add the following to note 4 after Moran v. Burbine:

The Second Circuit distinguished *Guarno* in United States v. Anderson, 929 F.2d 96 (2d Cir.1991), in which it addressed the admissibility of a confession obtained after an officer had told a suspect that he had to choose between having a lawyer present during questioning and cooperating with the government. This was false, the court reasoned, since defendants who have acquired counsel commonly agree to cooperate with the government. Under a totality of the circumstances analysis, this rendered the confession given in *Anderson* involuntary. Distinguishing *Guarno,* the court emphasized that in that case the interrogation had not been custodial in nature:

> The obvious differences between *Guarno* and this case are that in that case the defendant was never arrested and read his *Miranda* warnings and the police made no false and/or misleading statements to *Guarno.* Here, the opposite is true. Hence, *Guarno* is inapposite.

929 F.2d at 102.

5. IMPACT OF *MIRANDA* AND EFFORTS AT LEGISLATIVE CHANGE

Page 522. Add the following to note 1 after 18 U.S.C.A. § 3501:

During oral argument in United States v. Green, ___ U.S. ___, 113 S.Ct. 1835, 123 L.Ed.2d 260 (1993) (per curiam), Chief Justice Rehnquist and Justice Scalia pressed the Government on why it was not relying upon 18 U.S.C.A. § 3501. Justice Scalia commented that although he had been listening to *Miranda* cases for seven terms as a member of the Court, the Government had never in any of those cases relied upon the statute although it was "certainly very relevant * * * to a lot of [those] cases." When asked by one member of the Court whether the Government ever relies upon the statute in the lower courts, counsel for the Government responded, "I'm not aware that we have taken the position that the statute does overrule the need for the *Miranda* warnings." Justice Scalia inquired whether the Government's practice of failing to rely on the statute constitute "sort of executive nullification of a congressional statute?" Obviously unenthusiastic about discussing the statute and the Government's failure to rely upon it in *Green,* counsel for the Government stressed that its failure to raise the statute in the lower courts precluded reliance on it before the Supreme Court. He added:

> [I]n cases like this[,] * * * we believe [admission of the confession is] consistent with *Miranda* * * *. [S]o, there's no need to take what would be the ultimate fall-back position that it doesn't matter that it violated *Miranda* because the statute says *Miranda* is no longer good law.

Transcript of Oral Argument, at 19–21.

In Davis v. United States, ___ U.S. ___, ___ n. *, 114 S.Ct. 2350, 2354 n. *, 129 L.Ed.2d 362, 370 n. * (1994), discussed in the material supplementing page 491 of the text, the Court declined the invitation of some amici to consider 18 U.S.C.A. § 3501, explaining that the Government had not relied upon the statute. Justice Scalia concurred in an opinion expressing frustration with the Government's continuing failure to rely on section 3501. "[W]ith limited exceptions," he noted, "the provision has been studiously avoided by every Administration, not only in this court but in the lower courts, since its enactment more than 25 years ago." He then added:

> [T]he refusal to consider arguments not raised is a sound prudential practice, rather than a statutory or constitutional mandate, and there are times when prudence dictates the contrary. As far as I am concerned, such a time will have arrived when a case that comes within the terms of this statute is next presented to us.
>
> For most of this century, voluntariness vel non was the touchstone of admissibility of confessions. Section 3501 of Title 18 seems to provide for that standard in federal criminal prosecutions today. I say "seems" because I do not wish to prejudge any issue of law. I am entirely open to the argument that § 3501 does not mean what it appears to say; that it is inapplicable for some other reason; or even that it is unconstitutional. But I will no longer be open to the argument that this Court should continue to ignore the commands of § 3501 simply because the Executive declines to insist that we observe them.

The Executive has the power (whether or not it has the right) effectively to nullify some provisions of law by the mere failure to prosecute—the exercise of so-called prosecutorial discretion. And it has the power (whether or not it has the right) to avoid application of § 3501 by simply declining to introduce into evidence confessions admissible under its terms. But once a prosecution has been commenced and a confession introduced, the Executive assuredly has neither the power nor the right to determine what objections to admissibility of the confession are valid in law. Section 3501 of Title 18 is a provision of law directed to the courts, reflecting the people's assessment of the proper balance to be struck between concern for persons interrogated in custody and the needs of effective law enforcement. We shirk our duty if we systematically disregard that statutory command simply because the Justice Department systematically declines to remind us of it.

The United States' repeated refusal to invoke § 3501, combined with the courts' traditional (albeit merely prudential) refusal to consider arguments not raised, has caused the federal judiciary to confront a host of "*Miranda*" issues that might be entirely irrelevant under federal law. Worse still, it may have produced—during an era of intense national concern about the problem of runaway crime—the acquittal and the nonprosecution of many dangerous felons, enabling them to continue their depredations upon our citizens. There is no excuse for this. Perhaps (though I do not immediately see why) the Justice Department has good basis for believing that allowing prosecutions to be defeated on grounds that could be avoided by invocation of § 3501 is consistent with the Executive's obligation to "take Care that the Laws be faithfully executed," U.S. Const., Art. II, § 3. That is not the point. The point is whether our continuing refusal to consider § 3501 is consistent with the Third Branch's obligation to decide according to the law. I think it is not.

___ U.S. at ___, 114 S.Ct. at 2358, 129 L.Ed.2d at 374–75 (Scalia, J., concurring).

Page 522. Add the following new note after 18 U.S.C.A. § 3501:

1a. In United States v. Alvarez–Sanchez, ___ U.S. ___, 114 S.Ct. 1599, 128 L.Ed.2d 319 (1994), the Supreme Court held that the provisions of 18 U.S.C.A. § 3501(c) are not triggered until a suspect has been arrested or detained for a federal offense. Thus where a suspect is in state custody, there has been no delay in bringing that suspect before a federal magistrate even if the arresting officers believe the suspect has violated federal law and even if—as in *Alvarez–Sanchez*—during that state custody the suspect is interrogated by federal law enforcement officers. If the federal officers' interrogation produces a confession later offered in a federal prosecution, § 3501(c)—whatever it means—was not triggered and therefore can have no effect on the admissibility of that confession. Usually this approach will permit straightforward application, Justice Thomas explained for the Court. He added:

> [T]he parties identify one presumably rare scenario that might present some potential for confusion: namely, the situation that would arise if state or local authorities, acting in collusion with federal officers, were to arrest and detain someone in order to allow the federal agents to interrogate him in violation of his right to a prompt federal presentment. Long before the enactment of § 3501, we held that a confession obtained during such a period of detention must be suppressed if the defendant could demonstrate

> the existence of improper collaboration between federal and state or local officers. See Anderson v. United States, 318 U.S. 350, 63 S.Ct. 599, 87 L.Ed. 829 (1943). In this case, however, we need not address § 3501's effect, if any, on the rule announced in *Anderson.* The District Court concluded that there was "no evidence" that a "collusive arrangement between state and federal agents * * * caused [Alvarez–Sanchez'] confession to be made," and we see no reason to disturb that factual finding.

___ U.S. at ___, 114 S.Ct. at 1604–05, 128 L.Ed.2d at 329. Justice Stevens concurred only in the judgment, suggesting that the Court had no need to comment on the finding of no collusive arrangement and that whether state custody is the sole basis of a suspect's detention is more troublesome than the Court acknowledged. ___ U.S. at ___, 114 S.Ct. at 1605–06, 128 L.Ed.2d at 330–31 (Stevens, J., concurring in the judgment).

Justice Thomas' opinion for the Court also noted continuing questions concerning the effect of § 3501 on the *McNabb–Mallory* Rule, discussed in note 2 on pages 424–25 of the text:

> The parties argue at some length over the proper interpretation of subsections (a) and (c) of 18 U.S.C. § 3501, and, in particular, over the question whether § 3501(c) requires suppression of a confession that is made by an arrestee prior to presentment and more than six hours after arrest, regardless of whether the confession was voluntarily made. The Government contends that through § 3501, Congress repudiated the *McNabb–Mallory* rule in its entirety. Under this theory, § 3501(c) creates a safe harbor that prohibits suppression on grounds of pre-presentment delay if a confession is made within six hours following arrest, but says nothing about the admissibility of a confession given beyond that 6–hour period. The admissibility of such a confession, the Government argues, is controlled by § 3501(a), which provides that voluntary confessions "shall be admitted in evidence."
>
> * * * [R]espondent contends that § 3501(c) codified a limited form of the *McNabb–Mallory* rule—one that requires the suppression of a confession made before presentment but after the expiration of the safe harbor period. A contrary interpretation of § 3501(c), respondent argues, would render that subsection meaningless in the face of § 3501(a).

___ U.S. at ___, 114 S.Ct. at 1602–03, 128 L.Ed.2d at 326–27. Because it found § 3501(c) had not been triggered by the situation presented, however, the Court found no need to address this controversy regarding the effect of the statute where it applies. Justice Ginsburg, joined by Justice Blackmun, concurred to emphasize that the Court was not deciding "the effect of § 3501(c) of confessions obtained more than six hours after an arrest on federal charges." ___ U.S. at ___, 114 S.Ct. at 1605, 128 L.Ed.2d at 330 (Ginsburg, J., concurring).

C. SIXTH AMENDMENT RIGHT TO COUNSEL

Page 527. Add the following to the discussion in the Editors' Introduction of *Application of the* Edwards *Rule:*

But the *Edwards* rule as applied in some Sixth Amendment situations has less impact than it has when applied in *Miranda* contexts. If a suspect invokes the right to counsel during police questioning to which *Miranda* applies, *Edwards* as construed in *Roberson* (see text at pages 488–89) means that officers cannot reapproach the suspect until a lawyer is present even if the subject of their concerns is a different offense. In McNeil v. Wisconsin, 501 U.S. 171, 111 S.Ct. 2204, 115 L.Ed.2d 158 (1991), the Supreme Court held that in the Sixth Amendment context *Edwards* was not so broad.

McNeil had been arrested for a West Allis, Wisconsin, armed robbery. He was brought before a court commissioner on that charge and was represented by a public defender at this appearance. The Commissioner set bail and scheduled a preliminary examination. Subsequently, McNeil was approached by officers seeking to question him about a robbery-murder committed in Caledonia, Wisconsin. After the officers warned McNeil under *Miranda,* he waived his rights and made several statements admitting participation in the Caledonia crimes. The Supreme Court assumed that the Sixth Amendment right to counsel attached by virtue of McNeil's court appearance and that by appearing with counsel McNeil invoked his Sixth Amendment right with regard to the West Allis robbery. McNeil claimed that under *Edwards* and *Roberson,* this meant that the officers were barred from reapproaching him concerning the Caledonia crimes.

Rejecting this, the majority explained that the Sixth Amendment right to counsel "is offense-specific." It does not attach until a prosecution is commenced. Its *Edwards* effect is similarly "offense-specific," and under Michigan v. Jackson (see text at pages 524–25) a suspect's invocation of the Sixth Amendment right to counsel does not bar officers from reapproaching the suspect regarding offenses as to which he does not yet have a Sixth Amendment right to counsel. McNeil "provided the statements at issue here before his Sixth Amendment right to counsel with respect to the Caledonia offenses had been (or could have been) invoked," and therefore the Sixth Amendment did not bar the use of those statements. 501 U.S. at 176, 111 S.Ct. at 2208, 115 L.Ed.2d at 167.

Justice Stevens, joined by Justices Marshall and Blackmun, dissented. The majority's holding, Justice Stevens observed, means that a suspect who tells a police officer he wishes an attorney is protected from being reapproached concerning even other crimes, but no such protection is given a suspect who requests a lawyer from a judge. This, he argued, makes little sense. But this will generally make little difference, he continued. In light of the Court's holding, competent counsel appearing with their clients at preliminary proceedings can be expected to make statements on the record that their clients are invoking their Fifth Amendment right to representation as well as their Sixth Amendment right. This, he concluded, would trigger *Edwards* and *Roberson* and bar officers from—in the absence of counsel—reapproaching the defendants concerning other offenses. 501 U.S. at 183, 111 S.Ct. at 2212, 115 L.Ed.2d at 172 (Stevens, J., dissenting).

Chapter 8

UNDERCOVER INVESTIGATIONS

B. ENTRAPMENT

Page 555. Insert the following case after the Notes:

JACOBSON v. UNITED STATES

Supreme Court of the United States, 1992.
503 U.S. 540, 112 S.Ct. 1535, 118 L.Ed.2d 147.

JUSTICE WHITE delivered the opinion of the Court.

On September 24, 1987, petitioner Keith Jacobson was indicted for violating a provision of the Child Protection Act of 1984, which criminalizes the knowing receipt through the mails of a "visual depiction [that] involves the use of a minor engaging in sexually explicit conduct * * *." 18 U.S.C. § 2252(a)(2)(A). Petitioner defended on the ground that the Government entrapped him into committing the crime through a series of communications from undercover agents that spanned the 26 months preceding his arrest. Petitioner was found guilty after a jury trial. The Court of Appeals affirmed his conviction, holding that the Government had carried its burden of proving beyond reasonable doubt that petitioner was predisposed to break the law and hence was not entrapped.

Because the Government overstepped the line between setting a trap for the "unwary innocent" and the "unwary criminal," Sherman v. United States, 356 U.S. 369, 372, 78 S.Ct. 819, 821, 2 L.Ed.2d 848 (1958), and as a matter of law failed to establish that petitioner was independently predisposed to commit the crime for which he was arrested, we reverse the Court of Appeals' judgment affirming his conviction.

I

In February 1984, petitioner, a 56–year–old veteran-turned-farmer who supported his elderly father in Nebraska, ordered two magazines and a brochure from a California adult bookstore. The magazines, entitled Bare Boys I and Bare Boys II, contained photographs of nude preteen and teenage boys. The contents of the magazines startled petitioner, who testified that he had expected to receive photographs of "young men 18 years or older." On cross-examination, he explained his response to the magazines:

> "[PROSECUTOR]: [Y]ou were shocked and surprised that there were pictures of very young boys without clothes on, is that correct?
>
> "[JACOBSON]: Yes, I was.

> "[PROSECUTOR]: Were you offended?
>
> ***
>
> "[JACOBSON]: I was not offended because I thought these were a nudist type publication. Many of the pictures were out in a rural or outdoor setting. There was—I didn't draw any sexual connotation or connection with that."

The young men depicted in the magazines were not engaged in sexual activity, and petitioner's receipt of the magazines was legal under both federal and Nebraska law. Within three months, the law with respect to child pornography changed; Congress passed the Act illegalizing the receipt through the mails of sexually explicit depictions of children. In the very month that the new provision became law, postal inspectors found petitioner's name on the mailing list of the California bookstore that had mailed him Bare Boys I and II. There followed over the next 2½ years, repeated efforts by two Government agencies, through five fictitious organizations and a bogus pen pal, to explore petitioner's willingness to break the new law by ordering sexually explicit photographs of children through the mail.

The Government began its efforts in January 1985 when a postal inspector sent petitioner a letter supposedly from the American Hedonist Society, which in fact was a fictitious organization. The letter included a membership application and stated the Society's doctrine: that members had the "right to read what we desire, the right to discuss similar interests with those who share our philosophy, and finally that we have the right to seek pleasure without restrictions being placed on us by outdated puritan morality." Petitioner enrolled in the organization and returned a sexual attitude questionnaire that asked him to rank on a scale of one to four his enjoyment of various sexual materials, with one being "really enjoy," two being "enjoy," three being "somewhat enjoy," and four being "do not enjoy." Petitioner ranked the entry "[p]re-teen sex" as a two, but indicated that he was opposed to pedophilia.

For a time, the Government left petitioner alone. But then a new "prohibited mail specialist" in the Postal Service found petitioner's name in a file, and in May 1986, petitioner received a solicitation from a second fictitious consumer research company, "Midlands Data Research," seeking a response from those who "believe in the joys of sex and the complete awareness of those lusty and youthful lads and lasses of the neophite [sic] age." The letter never explained whether "neophite" referred to minors or young adults. Petitioner responded: "Please feel free to send me more information, I am interested in teenage sexuality. Please keep my name confidential."

Petitioner then heard from yet another Government creation, "Heartland Institute for a New Tomorrow" (HINT), which proclaimed that it was "an organization founded to protect and promote sexual freedom and freedom of choice. We believe that arbitrarily imposed legislative sanctions restricting your sexual freedom should be rescinded through the legislative process." The letter also enclosed a second survey. Petitioner indicated that his interest in "[p]reteen sex-homosexual" material was above average, but not high. In response to another question, petitioner wrote: "Not only sexual expression but freedom of the press is under attack. We must be ever vigilant to counter attack right wing fundamentalists who are determined to curtail our freedoms."

"HINT" replied, portraying itself as a lobbying organization seeking to repeal "all statutes which regulate sexual activities, except those laws which deal with violent behavior, such as rape. HINT is also lobbying to eliminate any legal definition of 'the age of consent'." These lobbying efforts were to be funded by sales from a catalog to be published in the future "offering the sale of various items which we believe you will find to be both interesting and stimulating." HINT also provided computer matching of group members with similar survey responses; and, although petitioner was supplied with a list of potential "pen pals," he did not initiate any correspondence.

Nevertheless, the Government's "prohibited mail specialist" began writing to petitioner, using the pseudonym "Carl Long." The letters employed a tactic known as "mirroring," which the inspector described as "reflect[ing] whatever the interests are of the person we are writing to." Petitioner responded at first, indicating that his interest was primarily in "male-male items." Inspector "Long" wrote back:

> "My interests too are primarily male-male items. Are you satisfied with the type of VCR tapes available? Personally, I like the amateur stuff better if its [sic] well produced as it can get more kinky and also seems more real. I think the actors enjoy it more."

Petitioner responded:

> "As far as my likes are concerned, I like good looking young guys (in their late teens and early 20's) doing their thing together."

Petitioner's letters to "Long" made no reference to child pornography. After writing two letters, petitioner discontinued the correspondence.

By March 1987, 34 months had passed since the Government obtained petitioner's name from the mailing list of the California bookstore, and 26 months had passed since the Postal Service had commenced its mailings to petitioner. Although petitioner had responded to surveys and letters, the Government had no evidence that petitioner had ever intentionally possessed or been exposed to child pornography. The Postal Service had not checked petitioner's mail to determine whether he was receiving questionable mailings from persons—other than the Government—involved in the child pornography industry.

At this point, a second Government agency, the Customs Service, included petitioner in its own child pornography sting, "Operation Borderline," after receiving his name on lists submitted by the Postal Service. Using the name of a fictitious Canadian company called "Produit Outaouais," the Customs Service mailed petitioner a brochure advertising photographs of young boys engaging in sex. Petitioner placed an order that was never filled.

The Postal Service also continued its efforts in the Jacobson case, writing to petitioner as the "Far Eastern Trading Company Ltd." The letter began:

> "As many of you know, much hysterical nonsense has appeared in the American media concerning 'pornography' and what must be done to stop it from coming across your borders. This brief letter does not allow us to give much comments; however, why is your government spending millions of dollars to exercise international censorship while tons of drugs, which makes yours the world's most crime ridden country are passed through easily."

The letter went on to say:

> "[W]e have devised a method of getting these to you without prying eyes of U.S. Customs seizing your mail * * *. After consultations with American solicitors, we have been advised that once we have posted our material through your system, it cannot be opened for any inspection without authorization of a judge."

The letter invited petitioner to send for more information. It also asked petitioner to sign an affirmation that he was "not a law enforcement officer or agent of the U.S. Government acting in an undercover capacity for the purpose of entrapping Far Eastern Trading Company, its agents or customers." Petitioner responded. A catalogue was sent, and petitioner ordered Boys Who Love Boys, a pornographic magazine depicting young boys engaged in various sexual activities. Petitioner was arrested after a controlled delivery of a photocopy of the magazine.

When petitioner was asked at trial why he placed such an order, he explained that the Government had succeeded in piquing his curiosity:

> "Well, the statement was made of all the trouble and the hysteria over pornography and I wanted to see what the material was. It didn't describe the—I didn't know for sure what kind of sexual action they were referring to in the Canadian letter * * *."

In petitioner's home, the Government found the Bare Boys magazines and materials that the Government had sent to him in the course of its protracted investigation, but no other materials that would indicate that petitioner collected or was actively interested in child pornography.

Petitioner was indicted * * *. The trial court instructed the jury on the petitioner's entrapment defense [and] petitioner was convicted * * *.

II

There can be no dispute about the evils of child pornography or the difficulties that laws and law enforcement have encountered in eliminating it. Likewise, there can be no dispute that the Government may use undercover agents to enforce the law. "It is well settled that the fact that officers or employees of the Government merely afford opportunities or facilities for the commission of the offense does not defeat the prosecution. Artifice and stratagem may be employed to catch those engaged in criminal enterprises." Sorrells v. United States, 287 U.S. 435, 441, 53 S.Ct. 210, 212, 77 L.Ed. 413 (1932).

In their zeal to enforce the law, however, Government agents may not originate a criminal design, implant in an innocent person's mind the disposition to commit a criminal act, and then induce commission of the crime so that the Government may prosecute. Where the Government has induced an individual to break the law and the defense of entrapment is at issue, as it was in this case, the prosecution must prove beyond reasonable doubt that the defendant was disposed to commit the criminal act prior to first being approached by Government agents.[2]

Thus, an agent deployed to stop the traffic in illegal drugs may offer the opportunity to buy or sell drugs, and, if the offer is accepted, make an arrest on the spot or later. In such a typical case, or in a more elaborate "sting" operation involving government-sponsored fencing where the defendant is simply provided with the opportunity to commit a crime, the entrapment defense is of little use because the ready commission of the criminal act amply demonstrates the defendant's predisposition. Had the agents in this case simply offered petitioner the opportunity to order child pornography through the mails, and petitioner—who must be presumed to know the law—had promptly availed himself of this criminal opportunity, it is unlikely that his entrapment defense would have warranted a jury instruction.

But that is not what happened here. By the time petitioner finally placed his order, he had already been the target of 26 months of repeated

[2] Inducement is not at issue in this case. The Government does not dispute that it induced petitioner to commit the crime. The sole issue is whether the Government carried its burden of proving that petitioner was predisposed to violate the law before the Government intervened. The dissent is mistaken in claiming that this is an innovation in entrapment law and in suggesting that the Government's conduct prior to the moment of solicitation is irrelevant. The Court rejected these arguments five decades ago in *Sorrells,* when the Court wrote that the Government may not punish an individual "for an alleged offense which is the product of the creative activity of its own officials" and that in such a case the Government "is in no position to object to evidence of the activities of its representatives in relation to the accused * * *." 287 U.S., at 451, 53 S.Ct., at 216. Indeed, the proposition that the accused must be predisposed prior to contact with law enforcement officers is so firmly established that the Government conceded the point at oral argument, submitting that the evidence it developed during the course of its investigation was probative because it indicated petitioner's state of mind prior to the commencement of the Government's investigation. * * *

mailings and communications from Government agents and fictitious organizations. Therefore, although he had become predisposed to break the law by May 1987, it is our view that the Government did not prove that this predisposition was independent and not the product of the attention that the Government had directed at petitioner since January 1985.

The prosecution's evidence of predisposition falls into two categories: evidence developed prior to the Postal Service's mail campaign, and that developed during the course of the investigation. The sole piece of preinvestigation evidence is petitioner's 1984 order and receipt of the Bare Boys magazines. But this is scant if any proof of petitioner's predisposition to commit an illegal act, the criminal character of which a defendant is presumed to know. It may indicate a predisposition to view sexually-oriented photographs that are responsive to his sexual tastes; but evidence that merely indicates a generic inclination to act within a broad range, not all of which is criminal, is of little probative value in establishing predisposition.

Furthermore, petitioner was acting within the law at the time he received these magazines. Receipt through the mails of sexually explicit depictions of children for noncommercial use did not become illegal under federal law until May 1984, and Nebraska had no law that forbade petitioner's possession of such material until 1988. Evidence of predisposition to do what once was lawful is not, by itself, sufficient to show predisposition to do what is not illegal, for there is a common understanding that most people obey the law even when they disapprove of it. This obedience may reflect a generalized respect for legality or the fear of prosecution, but for whatever reason, the law's prohibitions are matters of consequence. Hence, the fact that petitioner legally ordered and received the Bare Boys magazines does little to further the Government's burden of proving that petitioner was predisposed to commit a criminal act. This is particularly true given petitioner's unchallenged testimony was that he did not know until they arrived that the magazines would depict minors.

The prosecution's evidence gathered during the investigation also fails to carry the Government's burden. Petitioner's responses to the many communications prior to the ultimate criminal act were at most indicative of certain personal inclinations, including a predisposition to view photographs of preteen sex and a willingness to promote a given agenda by supporting lobbying organizations. Even so, petitioner's responses hardly support an inference that he would commit the crime of receiving child pornography through the mails.[3] * * *

[3] We do not hold, as the dissent suggests, that the Government was required to prove that petitioner knowingly violated the law. We simply conclude that proof that petitioner engaged in legal conduct and possessed certain generalized personal inclinations is not sufficient evidence to prove beyond a reasonable doubt that he would

On the other hand, the strong arguable inference is that, by waving the banner of individual rights and disparaging the legitimacy and constitutionality of efforts to restrict the availability of sexually explicit materials, the Government not only excited petitioner's interest in sexually explicit materials banned by law but also exerted substantial pressure on petitioner to obtain and read such material as part of a fight against censorship and the infringement of individual rights. * * *

Petitioner's ready response to these solicitations cannot be enough to establish beyond reasonable doubt that he was predisposed, prior to the Government acts intended to create predisposition, to commit the crime of receiving child pornography through the mails. The evidence that petitioner was ready and willing to commit the offense came only after the Government had devoted 2½ years to convincing him that he had or should have the right to engage in the very behavior proscribed by law. Rational jurors could not say beyond a reasonable doubt that petitioner possessed the requisite predisposition prior to the Government's investigation and that it existed independent of the Government's many and varied approaches to petitioner. * * *

Because * * * the prosecution failed, as a matter of law, to adduce evidence to support the jury verdict that petitioner was predisposed, independent of the Government's acts and beyond a reasonable doubt, to violate the law by receiving child pornography through the mails, we reverse the Court of Appeals' judgment affirming the conviction of Keith Jacobson.

It is so ordered.

JUSTICE O'CONNOR, with whom THE CHIEF JUSTICE and JUSTICE KENNEDY join, and with whom JUSTICE SCALIA joins except as to Part II, dissenting.

* * * I believe the Court fails to acknowledge the reasonableness of the jury's inference from the evidence, redefines "predisposition," and introduces a new requirement that Government sting operations have a reasonable suspicion of illegal activity before contacting a suspect.

I

This Court has held previously that a defendant's predisposition is to be assessed as of the time the Government agent first suggested the crime, not when the Government agent first became involved. Until the Government actually makes a suggestion of criminal conduct, it could not be said to have "implant[ed] in the mind of an innocent person the disposition to commit the alleged offense and induce its commission * * *." Sorrells v. United States, 287 U.S. 435, 442, 53 S.Ct. 210, 212–213, 77 L.Ed. 413 (1932). * * *

have been predisposed to commit the crime charged independent of the Government's coaxing.

Today, the Court holds that Government conduct may be considered to create a predisposition to commit a crime, even before any Government action to induce the commission of the crime. In my view, this holding changes entrapment doctrine. Generally, the inquiry is whether a suspect is predisposed before the Government induces the commission of the crime, not before the Government makes initial contact with him. There is no dispute here that the Government's questionnaires and letters were not sufficient to establish inducement; they did not even suggest that Mr. Jacobson should engage in any illegal activity. If all the Government had done was to send these materials, Mr. Jacobson's entrapment defense would fail. Yet the Court holds that the Government must prove not only that a suspect was predisposed to commit the crime before the opportunity to commit it arose, but also before the Government came on the scene.

The rule that preliminary Government contact can create a predisposition has the potential to be misread by lower courts as well as criminal investigators as requiring that the Government must have sufficient evidence of a defendant's predisposition before it ever seeks to contact him. Surely the Court cannot intend to impose such a requirement, for it would mean that the Government must have a reasonable suspicion of criminal activity before it begins an investigation, a condition that we have never before imposed. The Court denies that its new rule will affect run-of-the-mill sting operations, and one hopes that it means what it says. Nonetheless, after this case, every defendant will claim that something the Government agent did before soliciting the crime "created" a predisposition that was not there before. For example, a bribe taker will claim that the description of the amount of money available was so enticing that it implanted a disposition to accept the bribe later offered. A drug buyer will claim that the description of the drug's purity and effects was so tempting that it created the urge to try it for the first time. In short, the Court's opinion could be read to prohibit the Government from advertising the seductions of criminal activity as part of its sting operation, for fear of creating a predisposition in its suspects. * * *

II

The second puzzling thing about the Court's opinion is its redefinition of predisposition. The Court acknowledges that "[p]etitioner's responses to the many communications prior to the ultimate criminal act were * * * indicative of certain personal inclinations, including a predisposition to view photographs of preteen sex * * *." If true, this should have settled the matter; Mr. Jacobson was predisposed to engage in the illegal conduct. Yet, the Court concludes, "petitioner's responses hardly support an inference that he would commit the crime of receiving child pornography through the mails."

The Court seems to add something new to the burden of proving predisposition. Not only must the Government show that a defendant was predisposed to engage in the illegal conduct, here, receiving photographs of minors engaged in sex, but also that the defendant was predisposed to break the law knowingly in order to do so. The statute violated here, however, does not require proof of specific intent to break the law; it requires only knowing receipt of visual depictions produced by using minors engaged in sexually explicit conduct. Under the Court's analysis, however, the Government must prove more to show predisposition than it need prove in order to convict.

The Court ignores the judgment of Congress that specific intent is not an element of the crime of receiving sexually explicit photographs of minors. The elements of predisposition should track the elements of the crime. The predisposition requirement is meant to eliminate the entrapment defense for those defendants who would have committed the crime anyway, even absent Government inducement. Because a defendant might very well be convicted of the crime here absent Government inducement even though he did not know his conduct was illegal, a specific intent requirement does little to distinguish between those who would commit the crime without the inducement and those who would not. In sum, although the fact that Mr. Jacobson's purchases of Bare Boys I and Bare Boys II were legal at the time may have some relevance to the question of predisposition, it is not, as the Court suggests, dispositive.

* * * Because I believe there was sufficient evidence to uphold the jury's verdict, I respectfully dissent.

Chapter 9

GRAND JURY INVESTIGATIVE FUNCTIONS

A. THE SUBPOENA POWER

Page 593. Add the following new notes between notes 1 and 2 after United States v. Mara:

1a. Under Federal Rule of Criminal Procedure 17(c), a person served with a subpoena commanding the production of papers or other objects (a subpoena *duces tecum*) may move the court to quash or modify the subpoena on the grounds that "compliance would be unreasonable or oppressive." Application of the provision to grand jury subpoenas was addressed in United States v. R. Enterprises, Inc., 498 U.S. 292, 111 S.Ct. 722, 112 L.Ed.2d 795 (1991). A federal grand jury investigating allegations of interstate transportation of obscene materials had issued subpoenas to R. Enterprises and two other companies all owned by one Martin Rothstein; the subpoenas called for production of a variety of records. All three companies moved to quash the subpoenas, primarily on the ground that they called for material irrelevant to the grand jury's investigation; the district court denied the motions. The Court of Appeals, however, reversed. In United States v. Nixon, 418 U.S. 683, 94 S.Ct. 3090, 41 L.Ed.2d 1039 (1974), the Supreme Court held that a subpoena calling for production of documents before trial is to be enforced only if the party seeking it shows relevancy, admissibility and specificity. The Court of Appeals in *R. Enterprises* held that these standards were also applicable to grand jury subpoenas *duces tecum* and that those issued in the case did not meet the standards.

The Supreme Court reversed. Given the function of the grand jury, Justice O'Connor explained, the *Nixon* standards do not apply to grand jury subpoenas. Rule 17(c) imposes a requirement of "reasonableness" on grand jury subpoenas, she continued, and the Court's task was to fashion a standard for reasonableness in the context of grand jury proceedings:

> [T]he law presumes, absent a strong showing to the contrary, that a grand jury acts within the legitimate scope of its authority. Consequently, a grand jury subpoena issued through normal channels is presumed to be reasonable, and the burden of showing unreasonableness must be on the recipient who seeks to avoid compliance. * * * [W]here, as here, a subpoena is challenged on relevancy grounds, the motion to quash must be denied unless the district court determines that there is no reasonable possibility that the category of materials the Government seeks will produce information relevant to the general subject of the grand jury's investigation.

498 U.S. at 300–01, 111 S.Ct. at 728, 112 L.Ed.2d at 807–08. The subpoenas at issue had not been challenged as being too indefinite or as calling for overly burdensome production, the Court noted, and consequently the Court was not considering such claims.

A person served with a subpoena may not know the general subject matter of the grand jury's investigation, the Court observed, and therefore even if such a person has a valid claim to have the subpoena quashed they may not be able to make the showing necessary under the standard set out by the Court. Although it did not resolve the matter, the Court suggested that in a case where unreasonableness is alleged, the District Court might be justified in requiring the Government to reveal the general subject matter of the investigation before requiring the challenging party to carry its burden of persuasion with regard to unreasonableness. To discourage subpoena challenges as a means of achieving discovery, Justice O'Connor added, such disclosure might be required *in camera.* 498 U.S. at 301–02, 111 S.Ct. at 728–29, 112 L.Ed.2d at 808.

Turning to the facts of the case, the Court noted that all three companies were shown to have been owned by one person and to have done business in the same area. One of the three, further, had been shown to have shipped sexually explicit material into the district of concern to the grand jury. From these undisputed facts the District Court could have properly concluded that there was a reasonable possibility that the records would produce information relevant to the grand jury's investigation into the interstate transportation of obscene material. Thus the District Court correctly denied the motions to quash the subpoenas. 498 U.S. at 302–03, 111 S.Ct. at 729, 112 L.Ed.2d at 808–09.

1b. One court has held that a grand jury subpoena may not be used to compel a person to "produce" a sample of their blood. In Re Grand Jury Proceedings, 816 F.Supp. 1196, 1205 (W.D.Ky.1993):

> We hold that the United States' decision to seek T.S.'s blood sample with a grand jury subpoena was not an appropriate use of such a subpoena. To allow the United States to use a Rule 17(c) subpoena for this purpose would abrogate T.S.'s Fourth Amendment rights and, thus, transform the subpoena into an instrument by which an illegal search and seizure is effectuated. This is a result clearly not intended under the Federal Rules of Criminal Procedure, the Fourth Amendment, or applicable Supreme Court precedent.
>
> Therefore, we conclude that the United States must obtain a warrant before we will compel T.S. to comply with the demand for blood samples. To do so, the United States must establish probable cause that T.S.'s blood samples will yield evidence of a crime.

Part Two
PROSECUTION AND ADJUDICATION

Chapter 11
THE INITIAL APPEARANCE AND DETENTION

Page 648. Add the following Note after Gerstein v. Pugh:

NOTE

Gerstein held that a judicial determination of probable cause must be made "either before or promptly after arrest." The opinion did not, however, define "promptly." In County of Riverside v. McLaughlin, 500 U.S. 44, 111 S.Ct. 1661, 114 L.Ed.2d 49 (1991), the respondent, by federal class action, challenged a practice in Riverside County, California in which persons arrested without a warrant received a judicial determination of probable cause at the arraignment or first appearance before the magistrate. The arraignment occurred within 2 days of arrest, excluding weekends and holidays. Thus, one arrested late in the week might be held as long as 5 days before probable cause was determined by the magistrate; in the case of the Thanksgiving holiday, a 7-day delay was possible. The United States District Court issued an injunction requiring that determinations of probable cause be made within 36 hours of warrantless arrests, absent exigent circumstances. This order was affirmed by the United States Court of Appeals. McLaughlin v. County of Riverside, 888 F.2d 1276 (9th Cir.1989) cert. granted 498 U.S. 808, 111 S.Ct. 40, 112 L.Ed.2d 16 (1990).

The Supreme Court, in an opinion by Justice O'Connor, vacated the judgment of the Court of Appeals. The Ninth Circuit had erroneously interpreted *Gerstein* to require a determination of probable cause as soon as the administrative steps incident to arrest—fingerprinting, photographing, searching—were completed. This did not sufficiently allow for variations in state procedures and in particular did not take into account the need in some states to combine the *Gerstein* determination with the initial appearance before the magistrate. The Court concluded that "a jurisdiction that provides judicial determinations of probable cause within 48 hours of arrest will, as a general matter, comply with the promptness requirement of *Gerstein.*" A determination may not be prompt, however, even if within the 48 hour guideline if it was delayed unreasonably, such as a delay to gather additional evidence to justify the arrest, a delay motivated by ill will against the arrestee, or a delay for delay's sake. Conversely, if the determination is made later than 48 hours after arrest, the burden is upon the government to justify it by showing "the existence of a bona fide emergency or other extraordinary circumstance." The Court made it clear that a desire to combine the probable cause determination with other pretrial proceedings will not justify delay beyond 48 hours, nor will intervening weekends.

Justice Marshall, joined by Justices Blackmun and Stevens, dissented, agreeing with the Court of Appeals that a *Gerstein* determination is required as soon as the administrative steps incident to arrest are completed. Justice Scalia dissented on the ground that any delay beyond 24 hours should create a presumption of unreasonableness requiring governmental rebuttal. This, he believed, was required by the historical common law requirement of prompt presentation to the magistrate following arrest.

In Powell v. Nevada, ___ U.S. ___, 114 S.Ct. 1280, 128 L.Ed.2d 1 (1994), Petitioner was arrested without a warrant and held for four days before being presented to a magistrate. At his trial for murder, a statement made by Petitioner on the fourth day after his arrest was introduced into evidence. The Nevada Supreme Court held that the 48 hour rule of McLaughlin did not apply because Petitioner's prosecution began before McLaughlin was decided. The Supreme Court vacated that judgment on the ground that McLaughlin applies to all cases not yet final when the rule was announced. However, the Court noted Petitioner does not necessarily have to be re-tried because the Nevada Supreme Court had not considered the question what remedy is appropriate for a McLaughlin violation, which is a question the Court has not yet decided. What remedies would be appropriate? Could they ever include excluding a statement made during a period of detention in violation of McLaughlin's requirement of presentment within 48 hours?

Chapter 14

THE PRELIMINARY EXAMINATION AND THE GRAND JURY

A. THE PRELIMINARY HEARING

Page 728. Add the following Note to the Notes after Myers v. Commonwealth:

8. The California preliminary hearing or examination, discussed in note 7 of the text, was dramatically changed by an initiative measure—Proposition 115 or the "Crime Victims Justice Reform Act"—adopted in 1990 by the voters of that state. The measure affected both statutory and constitutional provisions. Perhaps the purpose of the changes is best reflected in section 866 of the California Penal Code as amended by the measure:

> It is the purpose of a preliminary examination to establish whether there exists probable cause to believe that the defendant has committed a felony. The examination shall not be used for purposes of discovery.

Moreover, the availability of preliminary examinations was reduced by providing in article I, section 14.1 of the California Constitution: "If a felony is prosecuted by indictment, there shall be no postindictment preliminary hearing."

To implement the voters' obvious desire to reduce the impact of preliminary examinations upon crime victims, article I, section 30 of the Constitution was amended by Proposition 115 to add the following:

> In order to protect victims and witnesses in criminal cases, hearsay evidence shall be admissible at preliminary hearings, as prescribed by the Legislature or by the people through the initiative process.

This was effectuated by amendment of Section 872(b) of the Penal Code to provide:

> Notwithstanding Section 1200 of the Evidence Code [the hearsay rule], the finding of probable cause may be based in whole or in part upon the sworn testimony of a law enforcement officer relating the statements of declarants made out of court offered for the truth of the matter asserted. Any law enforcement officer testifying as to hearsay statements shall either have five years of law enforcement experience or have completed a training course certified by the Commission on Peace Officer Standards and Training which includes training in the investigation and reporting of cases and testifying at preliminary hearings.

Section 1203 of California's Evidence Code requires that all hearsay declarants be made available for cross-examination. The 1990 initiative enacted section 1203.1, which provides:

> Section 1203 is not applicable if the hearsay statement is offered at a preliminary examination, as provided in Section 872 of the Penal Code.

A defendant's right to call witnesses at the preliminary examination was also limited by amendment of Penal Code section 866, subdivision (a) to provide:

> Upon the request of the prosecuting attorney, the magistrate shall require an offer of proof from the defense as to the testimony expected from [a defense] witness. The magistrate shall not permit the testimony of any defense witness unless the offer of proof discloses to the satisfaction of the magistrate, in his or her discretion, that the testimony of that witness, if believed, would be reasonably likely to establish an affirmative defense, negate an element of a crime charged, or impeach the testimony of a prosecution witness or the statement of a declarant testified to by a prosecution witness.

As the California Supreme Court commented in Whitman v. Superior Court (People), 54 Cal.3d 1063, 2 Cal.Rptr.2d 160, 820 P.2d 262 (1991):

> [Section 866, as amended by the initiative] marks a sharp contrast to this court's previous expansive concept of the preliminary hearing as a discovery and trial preparation device, allowing counsel the opportunity to "fashion" their impeachment tools for use in cross-examination at trial, to preserve testimony favorable to the defense, and to provide the defense "with valuable information about the case against the accused, enhancing its ability to evaluate the desirability of entering a plea or to prepare for trial."

54 Cal.3d at 1072–73, 2 Cal.Rptr.2d at 164–65, 820 P.2d at 272, quoting from Hawkins v. Superior Court, 22 Cal.3d 584, 588, 150 Cal.Rptr. 435, 437, 586 P.2d 916, 918 (1978), discussed in note 7, supra.

The California Supreme Court recognized that the enactment of article I, section 14.1 of the California Constitution negated its earlier holding in *Hawkins* that the state Equal Protection Clause gave an indicted felony defendant a right to a preliminary examination. It also held that granting preliminary examinations to only nonindicted defendants does not violate the Equal Protection Clause of the Fourteenth Amendment. Bowens v. Superior Court (People), 1 Cal.4th 36, 2 Cal.Rptr.2d 376, 820 P.2d 600 (1991).

In *Whitman,* supra, the court turned to the effect of the constitutional and statutory provisions permitting hearsay to be used by the prosecution. In *Whitman,* the only witness at the defendant's preliminary examination was a "reader" police officer, that is, an officer with the experience required by section 872(b) but who had no direct, personal knowledge of the offense or the investigation and simply read the report of the investigating officers. The voters' intention, held the court, was not to permit use of this sort of hearsay:

> Properly construed, Proposition 115 does not authorize a finding of probable cause based on the testimony of a noninvestigating officer or "reader" merely reciting the police report of an investigating officer. We believe the probable intent of the framers of the measure was to allow a properly qualified investigating officer to relate out-of-court statements by crime victims or witnesses, including other law enforcement personnel, without requiring the victims' or witnesses' presence in court. The testifying officer, however, must not be a mere reader but must have sufficient knowledge of the crime or the circumstances under which the out-of-court statement was made so as to meaningfully assist the magistrate in assessing the reliability of the statement.

54 Cal.3d at 1071–73, 2 Cal.Rptr.2d at 164–65, 820 P.2d at 266–67.

For a general discussion, see Berend, Proposition 115 Preliminary Hearings: Sacrificing Reliability on the Altar of Expediency, 23 Pacific L.J. 1131 (1992).

B. THE GRAND JURY

Page 735. Add the following to note 4 after Costello v. United States:

The Supreme Court considered federal prosecutors' duty to present exculpatory evidence to grand juries in United States v. Williams, 504 U.S. 36, 112 S.Ct. 1735, 118 L.Ed.2d 352 (1992). The Tenth Circuit had held, pursuant to what it regarded as the federal courts' "supervisory power," that federal prosecutors in possession of "substantial exculpatory evidence" concerning a suspect under consideration by a grand jury had a duty to present that evidence to the grand jury. Finding on the facts of *Williams* that the Government violated this duty and that there was at least a grave doubt as to whether the grand jury's decision to indict Williams was free from substantial influence by this violation, the lower courts required that Williams' indictment be dismissed. The Supreme Court reversed, and disapproved the Tenth Circuit's position. Federal grand juries, Justice Scalia explained for the Court, are "functionally independe[nt]" from the judicial branch, and therefore the federal judiciary has at most very limited supervisory power to fashion rules of procedure for grand jury proceedings. This limited power does not include the authority to promulgate rules that would "reshap[e] the grand jury institution." A rule requiring prosecutors to present exculpatory as well as incriminating evidence to grand juries would "alter the grand jury's historical role, transforming it from an accusatory to an adjudicatory body." The target of a grand jury investigation has no right to tender his "defense" to the grand jury. A grand jury can clearly refuse to hear exculpatory evidence. Federal courts cannot scrutinize the evidentiary support for a grand jury's decision to indict. Imposing upon a prosecutor a legal obligation to present to the grand jury exculpatory evidence in his possession would be incompatible with these aspects of the grand jury. If the courts will not review the evidentiary support for the grand jury's decision, for example, there is no sense in those same courts scrutinizing the prosecutor's presentation to the grand jury. Moreover, a target could "circumnavigate the system by delivering [his exculpatory evidence] to the prosecutor, whereupon it would have to be passed on to the grand jury * * *." The requirement applied to the case below by the Tenth Circuit, then, was beyond the authority of that court to develop pursuant to its inherent supervisory authority. Williams had not contended, Justice Scalia noted, that the Fifth Amendment itself compelled a rule requiring prosecutorial disclosure of exculpatory evidence to grand juries.

Four members of the Court dissented in an opinion by Justice Stevens. Grand juries, he reasoned, are subject to the control of the courts. The Supreme Court therefore has authority to create and enforce limited rules applicable in grand jury proceedings. Rules prohibiting prosecutorial misconduct are within this authority. Grand juries serve in part to protect citizens against arbitrary and oppressive governmental action. Prohibitions against prosecutorial misconduct—such as misleading grand juries—do not alter the traditional role of grand juries but merely assure their ability to perform one of their traditional functions. The nature of a grand jury proceeding precludes a rule requiring prosecutors to ferret out and present all evidence bearing on a suspect's guilt or innocence.

> But that does not mean that the prosecutor may mislead the grand jury into believing that there is probable cause to indict by withholding clear evidence to the contrary. I thus agree with the Department of Justice that "when a prosecutor conducting a grand jury inquiry is personally aware of substantial evidence which directly negates the guilt of a subject of the investigation, the prosecutor must present or otherwise disclose such evidence to the grand jury before seeking an indictment against such a person." U.S. Dept. of Justice, United States Attorneys' Manual, Title 9, ch. 11, par. 9–11.233, 88 (1988).

___ U.S. at ___, 112 S.Ct. at 1754, 118 L.Ed.2d at 379 (Stevens, J., dissenting). To enforce this, he concluded, the federal courts have the power to dismiss indictments because the prosecutor violated this duty.

Chapter 15

RIGHT TO A SPEEDY TRIAL

A. SIXTH AMENDMENT SPEEDY TRIAL GUARANTEE

Page 749. Add the following to Notes:

1a. The question how the fourth *Barker* factor—prejudice to the defense—should be analyzed was addressed by the Court in Doggett v. United States, ___ U.S. ___, 112 S.Ct. 2686, 120 L.Ed.2d 520 (1992). In 1980, Doggett was indicted on a federal drug conspiracy charge. When officers sought to arrest him three weeks later, they were told by his mother that he had left for Colombia four days earlier. The arrest warrant was entered on various law enforcement computer databases, including NCIC, but no further steps of substance were taken to apprehend him. In 1982, Doggett returned to the United States, married, earned a college degree, found a steady job as a computer operations manager, lived openly under his own name, and stayed within the law. In 1988, federal marshals ran a credit check on several thousand persons wanted on arrest warrants and discovered Doggett's whereabouts. He was promptly located and arrested. Doggett filed a motion to dismiss the indictment for speedy trial violation.

The United States District Court denied Doggett's speedy trial claim. He entered a conditional plea of guilty and appealed. The Eleventh Circuit affirmed the conviction. The United States Supreme Court, in an opinion by Justice Souter, reversed.

The length of the delay was well over the presumptively prejudicial one year delay. As to the reason for the delay, the government was negligent in failing to apprehend him at least during the 6 year period when he was living openly under his own name in the United States. As to prompt assertion of the right to a speedy trial, Doggett claimed that he did not know of the indictment until his arrest in 1988 and in the stipulation entered with the guilty plea, the government conceded it had no contradictory information.

As to prejudice from the delay, Doggett was unable to show that his defense was prejudiced from lost exculpatory evidence. However, "excessive delay presumptively compromises the reliability of a trial in ways that neither party can prove or, for that matter, identify." If the government had used diligence in apprehending Doggett, he would have been required to show actual prejudice to prevail. On the other hand, if Doggett could have shown intentional delay by the government to obtain a tactical advantage, no showing of prejudice at all would have been required of him. The delay here was neither, but was negligent. The Court concluded,

> Although negligence is obviously to be weighed more lightly than a deliberate intent to harm the accused's defense, it still falls on the wrong side of the divide between acceptable and unacceptable reasons for delaying a criminal prosecution once it has begun. And such is the nature of the

> prejudice presumed that the weight we assign to official negligence compounds over time as the presumption of evidentiary prejudice grows. Thus, our toleration of such negligence varies inversely with its protractedness * * * and its consequent threat to the fairness of the accused's trial. Condoning prolonged and unjustifiable delays in prosecution would both penalize many defendants for the state's fault and simply encourage the government to gamble with the interests of criminal suspects assigned a low prosecutorial priority. The Government, indeed, can hardly complain too loudly, for persistent neglect in concluding a criminal prosecution indicates an uncommonly feeble interest in bringing an accused to justice; the more weight the Government attaches to securing a conviction, the harder it will try to get it.
>
> [T]o warrant granting relief, negligence unaccompanied by particularized trial prejudice must have lasted longer than negligence demonstrably causing such prejudice * * *. When the Government's negligence * * * causes delay six times as long as that generally sufficient to trigger judicial review * * * and when the presumption of prejudice, albeit unspecified, is neither extenuated, as by the defendant's acquiescence, * * * nor persuasively rebutted, the defendant is entitled to relief.

___ U.S. at ___, 112 S.Ct. at 2693–94, 120 L.Ed.2d at 531–32. Justice O'Connor, dissenting, characterized the harm to Doggett from the delay as "speculative." She also noted that the delay harmed the Government's ability to discharge its burden of proof. Justice Thomas, joined by The Chief Justice and Justice Scalia, dissented on the ground that the Sixth Amendment guarantee of a speedy trial does not protect against prejudice to the defense.

Page 751. Add the following before Note 5:

4a. The Sixth Amendment issues discussed by Smith v. Hooey are also dealt with by the Interstate Agreement on Detainers, enacted by the United States and 48 states. Under the Agreement, a prisoner in one member state has a right to be tried by another member state "within one hundred and eighty days after he shall have caused to be delivered" to the state filing the charges a demand for a speedy trial. Failure to observe the time requirement results in dismissal of the charges with prejudice. In Fex v. Michigan, ___ U.S. ___, 113 S.Ct. 1085, 122 L.Ed.2d 406 (1993), the Supreme Court, in an opinion by Justice Scalia, held that the 180 day time period begins to run from the time the demand is received by the court and prosecutor in the State in which the charges had been filed, rather than from the time the prisoner gave the demand to his warden for transmittal. The opinion, based largely on textual analysis, also concluded that the burdens of non-deliverance of the demand or of delay in deliverance under the Court's interpretation were less than the burdens imposed on society should the petitioner's position be adopted. The latter might result in preclusion of prosecution in a case in which the prosecutor had received no timely notice of demand or even no notice at all of demand. Justice Blackmun, joined by Justice Stevens, dissented.

Chapter 16

COMPETENCY TO STAND TRIAL

Page 765. Add the following at the end of the introductory text:

The Court returned to the criteria for determining competency in Godinez v. Moran, ___ U.S. ___, 113 S.Ct. 2680, 125 L.Ed.2d 321 (1993). Godinez shot and killed a bartender and a bar patron and then removed the bar's cash register. Nine days later, he shot and killed his former wife and then shot himself in the abdomen and slit his own wrists. Nevertheless, he survived and was charged with three counts of first degree murder. Two psychiatrists examined him. On the basis of their reports the trial judge found Godinez competent to stand trial. Godinez first pleaded not guilty, but then told the court that he wished to discharge his attorneys, represent himself, and plead guilty. After making a variety of inquiries of him, the court accepted both his waiver of counsel and his plea of guilty. Godinez was subsequently sentenced to death. Several years later, he filed a petition for post-conviction relief in the state court, which held a hearing and determined that he had been competent to represent himself. In subsequent federal habeas litigation, however, the Court of Appeals for the Ninth Circuit held the determinations that Godinez was competent did not adequately protect his federal constitutional rights. *Westbrook,* the court concluded, means that the competency of a defendant who waives counsel or pleads guilty must be determined by a higher standard than *Dusky* directs for assessing the competency of defendants who go to trial. A defendant who waives counsel or pleads guilty is competent, it reasoned, only if he has "the capacity for 'reasoned choice' among the alternatives available to him." Since no determination that Godinez had this capacity was made, his conviction and death sentence were held constitutionally invalid.

The Supreme Court reversed, reasoning that the Ninth Circuit had read too much into *Westbrook.* Justice Thomas explained the Court's position:

> [A]ll criminal defendants—not merely those who plead guilty—may be required to make important decisions once criminal proceedings have been initiated. And while the decision to plead guilty is undeniably a profound one, it is no more complicated than the sum total of decisions that a defendant may be called upon to make during the course of a trial. * * * This being so, we can conceive of no basis for demanding a higher level of competence for those defendants who choose to plead guilty. If the *Dusky* standard is

> adequate for defendants who plead not guilty, it is necessarily adequate for those who plead guilty.
>
> Nor do we think that a defendant who waives his right to the assistance of counsel must be more competent than a defendant who does not, since there is no reason to believe that the decision to waive counsel requires an appreciably higher level of mental functioning than the decision to waive other constitutional rights. * * *
>
> Requiring that a criminal defendant be competent has a modest aim: It seeks to ensure that he has the capacity to understand the proceedings and to assist counsel. While psychiatrists and scholars may find it useful to classify the various kinds and degrees of competence, and while States are free to adopt competency standards that are more elaborate than the *Dusky* formulation, the Due Process Clause does not impose these additional requirements.

___ U.S. at ___, 113 S.Ct. at 2686–88, 125 L.Ed.2d at 332–34. *Westbrook,* Justice Thomas commented, simply means that in some cases trial judges are obligated to both inquire into the defendants' competency using the *Dusky* standard and satisfy themselves that the defendants' waivers are both knowing and voluntary.

Justice Blackmun, joined by Justice Stevens, dissented. The competency of defendants such as Godinez, who seek to proceed without counsel, must be determined by a standard that demands that they have the capacity to appreciate their position and to make a rational choice regarding representation, he argued. *Dusky's* test, he concluded, does not assure this:

> [T]he standard for competence to stand trial is specifically designed to measure a defendant's ability to "consult with counsel" and to "assist in preparing his defense." A finding that a defendant is competent to stand trial establishes only that he is capable of aiding his attorney in making the critical decisions required at trial or in plea negotiations. The reliability or even relevance of such a finding vanishes when its basic premise—that counsel will be present—ceases to exist. The question is no longer whether the defendant can proceed with an attorney, but whether he can proceed alone and uncounselled. I do not believe we place an excessive burden upon a trial court by requiring it to conduct a specific inquiry into that question at the juncture when a defendant whose competency has already been questioned seeks to waive counsel and represent himself.

___ U.S. at ___, 113 S.Ct. at 2693–94, 125 L.Ed.2d at 341 (Blackmun, J., dissenting).

A. THE DUTY TO INQUIRE INTO COMPETENCY

Page 772. Add the following Note after Pate v. Robinson:

3. Constitutional limits upon the allocation and nature of the burden of proof regarding competency to stand trial were addressed in Medina v. California, ___ U.S. ___, 112 S.Ct. 2572, 120 L.Ed.2d 353 (1992). Medina had been charged with first degree murder and defense counsel asked for an inquiry into his competency to stand trial. Under California procedure, the issue was tried to a jury. The jury was instructed that a defendant is presumed competent and that Medina had the burden of proving his incompetency by a preponderance of the evidence. After the jury found Medina competent, trial proceeded, he was convicted, and the death penalty was assessed. Before the Supreme Court, he argued that the California presumption of competency and California's requirement that he prove competency by a preponderance of the evidence offended due process.

The appropriate standard, Justice Kennedy explained for the Court, is that applied in Patterson v. New York, 432 U.S. 197, 97 S.Ct. 2319, 53 L.Ed.2d 281 (1977), discussed on pages 1004–1006 of the text. Substantial deference must be given to legislative judgments, and a legislative decision does not violate due process unless it offends a "principle of justice so rooted in the traditions and conscience of our people as to be ranked as fundamental."

Applying that standard, the majority found no due process violation. There is no settled tradition as to the proper allocation of the burden of proof on competency, and "[c]ontemporary practice" of the states and the federal government is varied. Placement of the burden on the defendant does not "transgress[ ] any recognized principle of 'fundamental fairness' in operation." Medina argued that "psychiatry is an inexact science," and placing on him the burden of proof requires that he bear the risk of being required to stand trial as a result of an erroneous finding of competency. Rejecting this, the Court reasoned that defense counsel will often have the best access to information and evidence, even if the defendant's ability to participate is impaired. Justice Kennedy explained:

> The Due Process Clause does not * * * require a State to adopt one procedure over another on the basis that it may produce results more favorable to the accused. * * * [I]t is enough that the State affords the criminal defendant on whose behalf a plea of incompetence is asserted a reasonable opportunity to demonstrate that he is not competent to stand trial.

___ U.S. at ___, 112 S.Ct. at 2580, 120 L.Ed.2d at 367.

Justice Blackmun, joined by Justice Stevens, dissented:

> [T]he Due Process clause does not simply forbid the State from trying and convicting a person who is incompetent. It also demands adequate *anticipatory, protective procedures* to minimize the risk that an incompetent person will be convicted. * * * In my view, [the majority's approach] introduces a systematic and unacceptably high risk that persons will be tried and convicted who are unable to follow or participate in the proceedings determining their fate.

___ U.S. at ___, 112 S.Ct. at 2584, 120 L.Ed.2d at 371–72. He found three reasons why the majority's reliance upon defense counsel's access to information and evidence was inappropriate:

> First, while the defendant is in custody, the State itself obviously has the most direct, unfettered access to him and is in the best position to observe his behavior. * * *
>
> Second, a competency determination is primarily a medical and psychiatric determination * * * [I]t is the experts and not the lawyers who are credited as the "best-informed," and most able to gauge a defendant's ability to understand and participate in the legal proceedings affecting him.
>
> Third, * * * [defense counsel's] view will likely have no outlet in, or effect on, the competency determination. Unlike the testimony of medical specialists or lay witnesses, the testimony of defense counsel is far more likely to be discounted by the factfinder as self-interested and biased. Defense counsel may also be discouraged in the first place from testifying for fear of abrogating an ethical responsibility or the attorney-client privilege.

___ U.S. at ___, 112 S.Ct. at 2588, 120 L.Ed.2d at 376–77.

B. PROCESSING OF INCOMPETENT DEFENDANTS

Page 779. Add the following to the Notes:

3. If a defendant is determined to be incompetent to stand trial because of a mental illness, under what circumstances may the defendant be forced to take medication that may sufficiently reduce his symptoms to render him competent to stand trial? Whether federal constitutional considerations limit the states' ability to so medicate incompetent defendants seemed to be at issue in Riggins v. Nevada, ___ U.S. ___, 112 S.Ct. 1810, 118 L.Ed.2d 479 (1992). Riggins, charged with murder, was found incompetent to stand trial and then was treated with Mellaril, a powerful antipsychotic medication. He received 800 milligrams of the drug each day. Riggins was subsequently found to be competent and trial was scheduled. He moved to terminate his treatment with the Mellaril, contending that continued treatment infringed upon his freedom. He also argued that his continued treatment would affect his demeanor and mental state during trial and thus would interfere with his ability to offer an insanity defense, since it would deprive him of the ability to show the jurors his "true mental state." The trial court denied the motion. Riggins was tried, and testified in his own defense. The jury—rejecting his insanity defense—convicted him and set his punishment at death.

The Supreme Court held that even assuming that Riggins' treatment with the Mellaril was "medically appropriate," on the facts of the case this treatment denied Riggins a full and fair trial under Fourteenth Amendment due process. In Washington v. Harper, 494 U.S. 210, 110 S.Ct. 1028, 108 L.Ed.2d 178 (1990), the Court had held that the Fourteenth Amendment's due process clause limits a state's ability to involuntarily treat a prison inmate with antipsychotic drugs because such forcible medication "represents a substantial interference with that person's liberty." 494 U.S. at 229, 110 S.Ct. at 1041. Justice O'Connor explained for the *Riggins* Court:

> Under *Harper,* forcing antipsychotic drugs on a convicted prisoner is impermissible absent a finding of overriding justification and a determination of medical appropriateness. The Fourteenth Amendment affords at least as much protection to persons the State detains for trial. * * * Thus, once Riggins moved to terminate administration of antipsychotic medication, the State became obligated to establish the need for Mellaril and the medical appropriateness of the drug.
>
> Although we have not had occasion to develop substantive standards for judging forced administration of such drugs in the trial or pretrial settings, Nevada certainly would have satisfied due process if the prosecution had demonstrated and the District Court had found that treatment with antipsychotic medication was medically appropriate and, considering less intrusive alternatives, essential for sake of Riggins' own safety or the safety of others. Similarly, the State might have been able to justify medically appropriate, involuntary treatment with the drug by establishing that it could not obtain an adjudication of Riggins' guilt or innocence by using less intrusive means. We note that during the * * * hearing [in the state court] Riggins did not contend that he had the right to be tried without Mellaril if its discontinuation rendered him incompetent. The question whether a competent criminal defendant may refuse antipsychotic medication if cessation of medication would render him incompetent at trial is not before us.

___ U.S. at ___, 112 S.Ct. at 1815, 118 L.Ed.2d at 489–90.

The trial court had not made the findings that due process required.

> This error may well have impaired the constitutionally protected trial rights Riggins invokes. At the hearing to consider terminating medication, [one expert] suggested that the dosage administered to Riggins * * * could make him "uptight." [Another expert] testified that a patient taking 800 milligrams of Mellaril each day might suffer from drowsiness or confusion. It is clearly possible that such side effects impacted not just Riggins' outward appearance, but also the contents of his testimony on direct or cross examination, his ability to follow the proceedings, or the substance of his communication with counsel.

___ U.S. at ___, 112 S.Ct. at 1816, 118 L.Ed.2d at 490. Requiring Riggins to demonstrate actual prejudice, the Court concluded, would lead to speculation and thus the demonstration of "a strong possibility that Riggins' defense was impaired due to the administration of Mellaril" required that relief be granted. The constitutional error was not "cured" by Riggins' ability at trial to present expert testimony to the jury regarding the effects upon his demeanor of the Mellaril he was taking. This could not have had any impact upon the possibility that the drug affected Riggins' own testimony, his interaction with counsel, or his comprehension. "[A]n unacceptable risk of prejudice remained." ___ U.S. at ___, 112 S.Ct. at 1816, 118 L.Ed.2d at 491.

Justice Kennedy concurred in the judgment of the Court but wrote separately to express his view on the issue not reached by the Court. He reviewed the possible side effects of antipsychotic medications such as the Mellaril administered to Riggins and their possible effects upon defendants at trial. Insofar as the medication inhibits defendants' ability to react and respond to the proceedings and to demonstrate remorse and compassion, he observed, the drug may result in especially acute prejudice during the sentencing stage and in a capital case "may * * * be determinative of whether the offender lives or dies." He then concluded:

> In my view elementary protections against state intrusion require the State in every case to make a showing that there is no significant risk that the medication will impair or alter in any material way the defendant's capacity or willingness to react to the testimony at trial or to assist his counsel. Based on my understanding of the medical literature, I have substantial reservations that the State can make that showing. * * *
>
> If the State cannot render the defendant competent without involuntary medication, then it must resort to civil commitment, if appropriate, unless the defendant becomes competent through other means. If the defendant cannot be tried without his behavior and demeanor being affected in this substantial way by involuntary treatment, in my view the Constitution requires that society bear this cost in order to preserve the integrity of the trial process.

___ U.S. at ___, 112 S.Ct. at 1818, 1820, 118 L.Ed.2d at 493, 496 (Kennedy, J. concurring in the judgment).

Justice Thomas, joined in part by Justice Scalia, dissented, arguing that Riggins failed to establish that he was actually forced to take the Mellaril and that even if he was forced to take it, he failed to demonstrate that this deprived him of a "fair" trial. ___ U.S. at ___, 112 S.Ct. at 1821, 118 L.Ed.2d at 496 (Thomas, J., dissenting).

Chapter 17

DISCOVERY AND DISCLOSURE

A. PROSECUTORIAL DISCLOSURE

Page 786. Add the following Notes after Rule 16:

NOTES

1. Rule 16(a)(1)(A) was amended by the Court in 1991. As amended, the Rule provides:

> (A) *Statement of Defendant.* Upon request of a defendant the government shall disclose to the defendant and make available for inspection, copying, or photographing: any relevant written or recorded statements made by the defendant, or copies thereof, within the possession, custody or control of the government, the existence of which is known, or by the exercise of due diligence may become known, to the attorney for the government; that portion of any written record containing the substance of any relevant oral statement made by the defendant whether before or after arrest in response to interrogation by any person then known to the defendant to be a government agent; and recorded testimony of the defendant before a grand jury which relates to the offense charged. The government shall also disclose to the defendant the substance of any other relevant oral statement made by the defendant whether before or after arrest in response to interrogation by any person then known by the defendant to be a government agent if the government intends to use that statement at trial.

The Committee Note indicates that the amendments were intended to make discoverable a record of an oral statement whether the government intended to offer the statement at trial and the substance of any oral statement that the government intends to use at trial. The Committee Note also indicates that the standard of "intends to use * * * at trial" is broader than "intends to offer in evidence at the trial" in that it includes statements intended by the government to be used for impeachment purposes only. 111 S.Ct. 801–02.

2. In 1993, the Court added a new provision to Rule 16(a)(1):

> (E) *Expert Witness.* At the defendant's request, the government shall disclose to the defendant a written summary of testimony the government intends to use under Rules 702, 703, or 705 of the Federal Rules of Evidence during its case in chief at trial. This summary must describe the witnesses' opinions, the bases and reasons therefor, and the witnesses' qualifications.

The Advisory Committee's note to an earlier draft of the revision explained:

> The amendment * * * is intended to reduce the element of surprise which often results from unexpected expert testimony, reduce the need for continuances, and to provide the opponent with a fair opportunity to test the merits of the expert's testimony through focused cross-examination. * * *

With increased use of both scientific and nonscientific expert testimony, one of the most basic discovery needs is to learn that an expert is expected to testify. This is particularly important where the expert is expected to testify on matters which touch on new or controversial techniques or opinions. * * *

Preliminary Draft of Proposed Amendments, Committee Note to Proposed Amendment of Rule 16, 137 F.R.D. 417, 491 (1991).

1. CONSTITUTIONAL OBLIGATIONS

Page 799. Add the following to the Notes after United States v. Bagley:

4. *Bagley*'s materiality standard was addressed in some detail in Kyles v. Whitley, ___ U.S. ___, 115 S.Ct. 1555, 131 L.Ed.2d 490 (1995). Kyles sought federal habeas corpus relief from his Louisiana conviction and death sentence on the ground that the prosecution had failed to disclose a number of exculpatory matters. Discussing the federal constitutional law to be applied to Kyles' contention, the Court explained:

> Four aspects of materiality under *Bagley* bear emphasis. Although the constitutional duty is triggered by the potential impact of favorable but undisclosed evidence, a showing of materiality does not require demonstration by a preponderance that disclosure of the suppressed evidence would have resulted ultimately in the defendant's acquittal (whether based on the presence of reasonable doubt or acceptance of an explanation for the crime that does not inculpate the defendant). *Bagley's* touchstone of materiality is a "reasonable probability" of a different result, and the adjective is important. The question is not whether the defendant would more likely than not have received a different verdict with the evidence, but whether in its absence he received a fair trial, understood as a trial resulting in a verdict worthy of confidence. A "reasonable probability" of a different result is accordingly shown when the Government's evidentiary suppression "undermines confidence in the outcome of the trial." *Bagley,* 473 U.S., at 678, 105 S.Ct., at 3381.
>
> The second aspect of *Bagley* materiality bearing emphasis here is that it is not a sufficiency of evidence test. A defendant need not demonstrate that after discounting the inculpatory evidence in light of the undisclosed evidence, there would not have been enough left to convict. The possibility of an acquittal on a criminal charge does not imply an insufficient evidentiary basis to convict. One does not show a *Brady* violation by demonstrating that some of the inculpatory evidence should have been excluded, but by showing that the favorable evidence could reasonably be taken to put the whole case in such a different light as to undermine confidence in the verdict.
>
> Third, we note that * * * once a reviewing court applying *Bagley* has found constitutional error there is no need for further harmless-error review. Assuming arguendo that a harmless error enquiry were to apply, a *Bagley* error could not be treated as harmless, since "a reasonable probability that, had the evidence been disclosed to the defense, the result of the proceeding would have been different," necessarily entails the conclusion that the suppression must have had " 'substantial and injurious effect or

influence in determining the jury's verdict,'" Brecht v. Abrahamson, 507 U.S. ___, ___, 113 S.Ct. 1710, 1712, 123 L.Ed.2d 353 (1993) [(setting out the standard of harmlessness generally to be applied in habeas cases)], quoting Kotteakos v. United States, 328 U.S. 750, 776, 66 S.Ct. 1239, 1253, 90 L.Ed. 1557 (1946). * * *

The fourth and final aspect of *Bagley* materiality to be stressed here is its definition in terms of suppressed evidence considered collectively, not item-by-item. * * * [T]he Constitution is not violated every time the government fails or chooses not to disclose evidence that might prove helpful to the defense. We have never held that the Constitution demands an open file policy (however such a policy might work out in practice), and the rule in *Bagley* (and, hence, in *Brady*) requires less of the prosecution than the ABA Standards for Criminal Justice, which call generally for prosecutorial disclosures of any evidence tending to exculpate or mitigate.

While the definition of *Bagley* materiality in terms of the cumulative effect of suppression must accordingly be seen as leaving the government with a degree of discretion, it must also be understood as imposing a corresponding burden. On the one side, showing that the prosecution knew of an item of favorable evidence unknown to the defense does not amount to a *Brady* violation, without more. But the prosecution, which alone can know what is undisclosed, must be assigned the consequent responsibility to gauge the likely net effect of all such evidence and make disclosure when the point of "reasonable probability" is reached. This in turn means that the individual prosecutor has a duty to learn of any favorable evidence known to the others acting on the government's behalf in the case, including the police. But whether the prosecutor succeeds or fails in meeting this obligation (whether, that is, a failure to disclose is in good faith or bad faith, the prosecution's responsibility for failing to disclose known, favorable evidence rising to a material level of importance is inescapable.

The State of Louisiana would prefer an even more lenient rule. It pleads that some of the favorable evidence in issue here was not disclosed even to the prosecutor until after trial, and it suggested below that it should not be held accountable under *Bagley* and *Brady* for evidence known only to police investigators and not to the prosecutor. To accommodate the State in this manner would, however, amount to a serious change of course from the *Brady* line of cases. In the State's favor it may be said that no one doubts that police investigators sometimes fail to inform a prosecutor of all they know. But neither is there any serious doubt that "procedures and regulations can be established to carry [the prosecutor's] burden and to insure communication of all relevant information on each case to every lawyer who deals with it." Giglio v. United States, 405 U.S. 150, 154, 92 S.Ct. 763, 766, 31 L.Ed.2d 104 (1972). Since, then, the prosecutor has the means to discharge the government's *Brady* responsibility if he will, any argument for excusing a prosecutor from disclosing what he does not happen to know about boils down to a plea to substitute the police for the prosecutor, and even for the courts themselves, as the final arbiters of the government's obligation to ensure fair trials.

Short of doing that, we were asked at oral argument to raise the threshold of materiality because the *Bagley* standard "makes it difficult ...

> to know" from the "perspective [of the prosecutor at] trial ... exactly what might become important later on." The State asks for "a certain amount of leeway in making a judgment call" as to the disclosure of any given piece of evidence.
>
> Uncertainty about the degree of further "leeway" that might satisfy the State's request for a "certain amount" of it is the least of the reasons to deny the request. At bottom, what the State fails to recognize is that, with or without more leeway, the prosecution cannot be subject to any disclosure obligation without at some point having the responsibility to determine when it must act. Indeed, even if due process were thought to be violated by every failure to disclose an item of exculpatory or impeachment evidence (leaving harmless error as the government's only fallback), the prosecutor would still be forced to make judgment calls about what would count as favorable evidence, owing to the very fact that the character of a piece of evidence as favorable will often turn on the context of the existing or potential evidentiary record. Since the prosecutor would have to exercise some judgment even if the State were subject to this most stringent disclosure obligation, it is hard to find merit in the State's complaint over the responsibility for judgment under the existing system, which does not tax the prosecutor with error for any failure to disclose, absent a further showing of materiality. Unless, indeed, the adversary system of prosecution is to descend to a gladiatorial level unmitigated by any prosecutorial obligation for the sake of truth, the government simply cannot avoid responsibility for knowing when the suppression of evidence has come to portend such an effect on a trial's outcome as to destroy confidence in its result.
>
> This means, naturally, that a prosecutor anxious about tacking too close to the wind will disclose a favorable piece of evidence. This is as it should be. Such disclosure will serve to justify trust in the prosecutor as "the representative ... of a sovereignty ... whose interest ... in a criminal prosecution is not that it shall win a case, but that justice shall be done." Berger v. United States, 295 U.S. 78, 88, 55 S.Ct. 629, 633, 79 L.Ed. 1314 (1935). And it will tend to preserve the criminal trial, as distinct from the prosecutor's private deliberations, as the chosen forum for ascertaining the truth about criminal accusations. The prudence of the careful prosecutor should not therefore be discouraged.

___ U.S. at ___, 115 S.Ct. at 1565–69, 131 L.Ed.2d at 506–10.

In the course of concluding that on the complicated facts before it the nondisclosed information at issue was material under *Bagley,* the Court commented that undisclosed information that would have permitted "the effective impeachment of one eyewitness can call for a new trial even though the attack does not extend directly to others." ___ U.S. at ___, 115 S.Ct. at 1571, 131 L.Ed.2d at 513. This, Justice Scalia observed in dissent, "is the major contribution of today's opinion to *Brady* litigation." "[W]ith our endorsement," he continued, "it will surely be trolled past appellate courts in all future failure to disclose cases." ___ U.S. at ___, 115 S.Ct. at 1582, 131 L.Ed.2d at 528 (Scalia, J., dissenting). He disagreed with the majority's comments on the merits of the matter:

> The weakening of one witness's testimony does not weaken the unconnected testimony of another witness; and to entertain the possibility that the jury

> will give it such an effect is incompatible with the whole idea of a materiality standard, which presumes that the incriminating evidence that would have been destroyed by proper disclosure can be logically separated from the incriminating evidence that would have remained unaffected.

___ U.S. at ___, 115 S.Ct. at 1583, 131 L.Ed.2d at 528.

B. DISCLOSURE BY THE DEFENSE

Page 805. Insert the following in the Editors' Introduction after the provisions of Rule 16(b)(1) on this page:

In 1993, the Court added an additional provision to Rule 16(b)(1):

> (C) *Expert Witnesses.* If the defendant requests disclosure under subdivision (a)(1)(E) of this rule and the government complies, the defendant, at the government's request, must disclose to the government a written summary of testimony the defendant intends to use under Rules 702, 703 and 705 of the Federal Rules of Evidence as evidence at trial. This summary must describe the opinions of the witnesses, the bases and reasons therefor, and the witnesses' qualifications.

Page 810. Add the following Notes:

NOTES

1. The respondent in Michigan v. Lucas, 500 U.S. 145, 111 S.Ct. 1743, 114 L.Ed.2d 205 (1991) was charged with the rape of his former girlfriend. Under Michigan's rape shield law, evidence of the victim's prior sexual conduct was made inadmissible, subject to an exception for prior sexual acts between the defendant and the victim. For the exception to apply, the defendant was required to give notice of intent to present such evidence and an offer of proof within 10 days of his arraignment. The trial court would then conduct an in camera hearing to determine whether the proposed evidence would be admitted. Lucas failed to give the statutory notice but wished at trial to introduce his own testimony that he and the victim had had sexual intercourse prior to the incident on trial. The trial court refused to permit this testimony for failure to comply with the rape shield statute. The Michigan Court of Appeals reversed Lucas' conviction on the ground that as applied to prior sexual relations between the defendant and the victim the notice provision serves no useful purpose. The Supreme Court, in an opinion by Justice O'Connor, reversed the Court of Appeals. The Court found that the notice requirement

> permits a prosecutor to interview persons who know the parties and otherwise investigate whether such a prior relationship actually existed. When a prior sexual relationship is conceded, the notice-and-hearing procedure allows a court to determine in advance of trial whether evidence of the relationship "is material to a fact at issue in the case" and whether "its inflammatory or prejudicial nature outweigh[s] its probative value." [Quoting from the Michigan statute.]

500 U.S. at 150, 111 S.Ct. at 1747, 114 L.Ed.2d at 212. Citing United States v. Nobles and Taylor v. Illinois [Casebook p. 784], the Court held that the Michigan Court of Appeals

> erred in adopting a *per se* rule that Michigan's notice-and-hearing requirement violates the Sixth Amendment in all cases where it is used to preclude evidence of past sexual conduct between a rape victim and a defendant. The Sixth Amendment is not so rigid. The notice-and-hearing requirement serves legitimate state interests in protecting against surprise, harassment, and undue delay. Failure to comply with this requirement may in some cases justify even the severe sanction of preclusion.

500 U.S. at 152, 111 S.Ct. at 1748, 114 L.Ed.2d at 214. The Court remanded the case to the Michigan court to determine whether the state statute authorized preclusion and, if so, whether on these particular facts preclusion would violate the Sixth Amendment. Justice Stevens, joined by Justice Marshall, dissented. Justice Blackmun filed a concurring opinion.

2. In 1990, California voters approved an initiative measure—the Crime Victims Justice Reform Act or Proposition 115—that made numerous changes in the state's criminal justice system, often thus "overruling" decisions of the California Supreme Court. Among the changes made were modifications of discovery. Article I of the California Constitution was amended to add section 30, which provides in part:

> (c) In order to provide for fair and speedy trials, discovery in criminal cases shall be reciprocal in nature, as prescribed by the Legislature or by the people through the initiative process.

The initiative measure also added a new Chapter to the Penal Code. This chapter mandates discovery by both the defendant and the prosecution. With regard to disclosure by the defense, Section 1054.3 provides:

> The defendant and his or her attorney shall disclose to the prosecuting attorney:
>
> (a) The names and addresses of persons, other than the defendant, he or she intends to call as witnesses at trial, together with any relevant written or recorded statements of those persons, or reports of the statements of those persons, including any reports or statements of experts made in connection with the case, and including the results of physical or mental examinations, scientific tests, experiments, or comparisons which the defendant intends to offer in evidence at the trial.
>
> (b) Any real evidence which the defendant intends to offer in evidence at the trial.

Under section 1054.6, neither the defendant nor the prosecutor is required to disclose any materials or information which are work product as defined in section 2018 of the Code of Civil Procedure. Section 2018(c) defines "work product" as "[a]ny writing that reflects an attorney's impressions, conclusions, opinions, or legal research or theories * * *."

In Izazaga v. Superior Court (People), 54 Cal.3d 356, 285 Cal.Rptr. 231, 815 P.2d 304 (1991), the California Supreme Court acknowledged that Proposition 115 abrogated *Prudhomme* (discussed on pages 806–07 of the text) and its progeny; the disclosure required by section 1054.3, therefore, violated no California constitutional provision. 54 Cal.3d at 369–78, 285 Cal.Rptr. at 239–46, 815 P.2d at 312–18. Further, the court—relying on *Williams* and *Nobles*—rejected arguments that the disclosure requirements violated the Fifth Amendment to the United States Constitution. 54 Cal.3d at 365–69, 285 Cal.Rptr. at 236–39, 815

P.2d at 309–12. In addition, the court held that under *Nobles,* enforcement of the state provision would not violate defendants' Sixth Amendment right to effective assistance of counsel. It rejected Izazaga's effort to distinguish *Nobles* on the grounds that *Nobles* involved (a) disclosure during rather than before trial; and (b) disclosure only after the defense had "waived" protection by electing to make use of the specific evidence, *i.e.,* the investigator's report. The court also observed:

> [U]nder the new discovery chapter, a criminal defendant need disclose only those witnesses (and their statements) the defendant intends to call at trial. It is logical to assume that only those witnesses defense counsel *deems helpful to the defense* will appear on a defendant's witness list. The identity of damaging witnesses that the defense does not intend to call at trial need *not* be disclosed. Thus, there is nothing in the new discovery chapter that would penalize exhaustive investigation or otherwise chill trial preparation of defense counsel such that criminal defendants would be denied the right to effective assistance of counsel under the Sixth Amendment.

54 Cal.3d at 379, 285 Cal.Rptr. at 246, 815 P.2d at 319.

Chapter 18

RIGHT TO AN IMPARTIAL TRIAL

Page 820. Add the following after Note 1:

1a. The issue in Mu'Min v. Virginia, 500 U.S. 415, 111 S.Ct. 1899, 114 L.Ed.2d 493 (1991) was whether the Sixth and Fourteenth Amendments right to an impartial jury was violated by the refusal of the trial court to question members of the jury panel about the content of pretrial publicity they had acknowledged receiving concerning the case and the defendant. Mu'Min was charged with a murder committed when he escaped from a prison work detail. Publicity was extensive and included the fact that he was already serving a prison sentence for murder, that he had been six times rejected for parole, details of the murder for which he was serving the prison sentence, and indications that he had confessed to the murder with which he was now charged. Twenty-six prospective jurors appeared for voir dire. Sixteen acknowledged they had read or heard about the case. One of the 16 was excused for cause when he stated he could not be impartial in light of the publicity. Further voir dire was conducted in panels of 4 persons. Each person stated that he or she could be impartial and would wait until the entire case was presented before forming an opinion about defendant's guilt or innocence. Defense counsel asked the trial court to question members of the panel who had heard about the case as to the content of the information they had received. The trial court refused this request. Of the 12 persons who were the jury, 8 had read or heard something about the case. Mu'Min was convicted and received the death penalty. The Supreme Court, in an opinion by Chief Justice Rehnquist, held that the trial court's actions did not violate the 6th and 14th Amendments. The Court acknowledged that questioning concerning content would have enabled petitioner to exercise peremptory challenges more intelligently, but refused to make such questions a constitutional requirement because under Ross v. Oklahoma, 487 U.S. 81, 108 S.Ct. 2273, 101 L.Ed.2d 80 (1988) peremptory challenges are not required by the Constitution. Petitioner's reliance on Irvin v. Dowd is misplaced since in that case 8 of 12 jurors had formed an opinion from pretrial publicity as to guilt, while in this case although 8 of 12 had heard of the case none expressed an opinion as to guilt.

> Had the trial court in this case been confronted with the "wave of public passion" engendered by pretrial publicity that occurred in connection with Irvin's trial, the Due Process Clause of the Fourteenth Amendment might well have required more extensive examination of potential jurors than it undertook here. But the showings are not comparable; the cases differ both in the kind of community in which the coverage took place and in the extent of media coverage. Unlike the community involved in *Irvin,* the county in which petitioner was tried, Prince William, had a population in 1988 of 182,537, and this was one of nine murders committed in the county that year. It is a part of the metropolitan Washington statistical area, which has a population of over 3 million, and in which, unfortunately, hundreds of murders are committed each year. In *Irvin,* news accounts included details

of the defendant's confessions to 24 burglaries and six murders, including the one for which he was tried, as well as his unaccepted offer to plead guilty in order to avoid the death sentence. They contained numerous opinions as to his guilt, as well as opinions about the appropriate punishment. While news reports about Mu'Min were not favorable, they did not contain the same sort of damaging information. Much of the pretrial publicity was aimed at the Department of Corrections and the criminal justice system in general, criticizing the furlough and work release programs that made this and other crimes possible. Any killing that ultimately results in a charge of capital murder will engender considerable media coverage, and this one may have engendered more than most because of its occurrence during the 1988 Presidential campaign, when a similar crime committed by a Massachusetts inmate became a subject of national debate. But, while the pretrial publicity in this case appears to have been substantial, it was not of the same kind or extent as that found to exist in *Irvin.*

500 U.S. at 429–30, 111 S.Ct. at 1907, 114 L.Ed.2d at 508.

Justice Marshall, joined by Justices Blackmun and Stevens, dissented. Justice Kennedy dissented because "a juror's acknowledgement of exposure to pretrial publicity initiates a duty to assess that individual juror's ability to be impartial." That duty was not discharged in this case:

> The questions were asked of groups, and individual jurors attested to their own impartiality by saying nothing. I would hold * * * that when a juror admits exposure to pretrial publicity about a case, the court must conduct a sufficient colloquy with the individual juror to make an assessment of the juror's ability to be impartial. The trial judge should have substantial discretion in conducting the *voir dire,* but, in my judgment, findings of impartiality must be based on something more than the mere silence of the individual in response to questions asked *en masse.*

500 U.S. at 452, 111 S.Ct. at 1919, 114 L.Ed.2d at 523.

Page 823. Add the following before Note 4:

3a. The Supreme Court considered the constitutionality under the First Amendment of the use of bar disciplinary rules to restrict attorneys in making pre-trial comments concerning a case in Gentile v. State Bar of Nevada, 501 U.S. 1030, 111 S.Ct. 2720, 115 L.Ed.2d 888 (1991). The Supreme Court of Nevada had promulgated bar disciplinary rule 177 (almost identical to ABA Model Rule of Professional Conduct 3.6) concerning trial publicity:

> 1. A lawyer shall not make an extrajudicial statement that a reasonable person would expect to be disseminated by means of public communication if the lawyer knows or reasonably should know that it will have a substantial likelihood of materially prejudicing an adjudicative proceeding.
>
> 2. A statement referred to in subsection 1 ordinarily is likely to have such an effect when it refers to a civil matter triable to a jury, a criminal matter, or any other proceeding that could result in incarceration, and the statement relates to:
>
> > (a) the character, credibility, reputation or criminal record of a party, suspect in a criminal investigation or witness, or the identity of a witness, or the expected testimony of a party or witness;

(b) in a criminal case or proceeding that could result in incarceration, the possibility of a plea of guilty to the offense or the existence or contents of any confession, admission, or statement given by a defendant or suspect or that person's refusal or failure to make a statement;

(c) the performance or results of any examination or test or the refusal or failure of a person to submit to an examination or test, or the identity or nature of physical evidence expected to be presented;

(d) any opinion as to the guilt or innocence of a defendant or suspect in a criminal case or proceeding that could result in incarceration;

(e) information the lawyer knows or reasonably should know is likely to be inadmissible as evidence in a trial and would if disclosed create a substantial risk of prejudicing an impartial trial; or

(f) the fact that a defendant has been charged with a crime, unless there is included therein a statement explaining that the charge is merely an accusation and that the defendant is presumed innocent until and unless proven guilty.

3. Notwithstanding subsection 1 and 2(a-f), a lawyer involved in the investigation or litigation of a matter may state without elaboration:

(a) the general nature of the claim or defense; * * *

Gentile, a Las Vegas criminal defense attorney, called a press conference shortly after his client was arrested and charged with offenses arising out of four kilograms of cocaine and almost $300,000 in travelers' checks that were missing from a safety deposit box. The box had been used by police in an undercover operation and was part of a business—Western Vault Corporation—owned by petitioner's client. There was extensive local publicity concerning the case before and after the arrest and charge. Petitioner examined the rules of discipline before calling the press conference and refused to answer several questions at the conference on grounds to do so would violate those rules. At the conference petitioner stated that his client was innocent, that the likely thief was a police detective (whom he named) and that others who claimed to be victims of similar losses were rug dealers or convicted money launderers, who were working with police wrongfully to accuse his client. At trial six months later, petitioner's client was acquitted of all charges. The Nevada Bar then brought disciplinary proceedings, which resulted in the Nevada Supreme Court ultimately issuing a private reprimand against petitioner for violation of Rule 177. The United States Supreme Court reversed. The Court held, through Justice Kennedy, that the rules as interpreted by the Nevada Supreme Court, were void for vagueness. Petitioner was misled by the "safe harbor" provision of Rule 177(3)(a) into believing that his conduct at the press conference was protected from bar discipline:

> A lawyer seeking to avail himself of Rule 177(3)'s protection must guess at its contours. The right to explain the "general" nature of the defense without "elaboration" provides insufficient guidance because "general" and "elaboration" are both classic terms of degree. In the context before us, these terms have no settled usage or tradition of interpretation in law. The lawyer has no principle for determining when his remarks pass from the safe harbor of the general to the forbidden sea of the elaborated.

501 U.S. at ___, 111 S.Ct. at 2731, 115 L.Ed.2d at 906–07. Then Justice Kennedy, writing for himself and Justices Marshall, Blackmun and Stevens, concluded that the Rule as applied in this case violated the First Amendment because this is pure political speech and the same standards should be used to determine whether petitioner's speech was protected by the First Amendment as any other person's. While the standard of the rule—"substantial likelihood of materially prejudicing an adjudicative proceeding"—is acceptable under the First Amendment, its application to the facts of this case violated petitioner's First Amendment rights. Chief Justice Rehnquist, writing for the Court, held that lawyers can be held to a lesser standard of First Amendment protection than other persons:

> Lawyers representing clients in pending cases are key participants in the criminal justice system, and the State may demand some adherence to the precepts of that system in regulating their speech as well as their conduct * * *. Because lawyers have special access to information through discovery and client communications, their extrajudicial statements pose a threat to the fairness of a pending proceeding since lawyers' statements are likely to be received as especially authoritative * * *. We agree with the majority of the States that the "substantial likelihood of material prejudice" standard constitutes a constitutionally permissible balance between the First Amendment rights of attorneys in pending cases and the state's interest in fair trials.

501 U.S. at ___, 111 S.Ct. at 2744–45, 115 L.Ed.2d at 923. Chief Justice Rehnquist, writing for himself and for Justices White, Scalia and Souter, concluded that Rule 177 as applied in this case should not be held void for vagueness. Justice O'Connor, while joining in Justice Kennedy's opinion that the Rule was as applied void for vagueness, emphasized her belief that lawyers may be judged by lower First Amendment standards than other persons because "lawyers are officers of the court and, as such, may legitimately be subject to ethical precepts that keep them from engaging in what otherwise might be constitutionally protected speech."

Page 826. Add the following before Note 9:

8a. The Supreme Court addressed the scope of the federal recusal of judges statute in Liteky v. United States, ___ U.S. ___, 114 S.Ct. 1147, 127 L.Ed.2d 474 (1994). Petitioners were charged with destruction of government property, which involved a political protest at a military base. One of the Petitioners had previously been tried before the same judge on a similar charge. Based on the judge's actions in the previous trial, Petitioners made a motion to have the judge recused under 28 U.S.C. § 455(a), which requires a federal judge to "disqualify himself in any proceeding in which his impartiality might reasonably be questioned." The motion was denied and the Petitioners were convicted. The Court of Appeals affirmed on the ground that "matters arising out of the course of judicial proceedings are not a proper basis for recusal." The Supreme Court, in an opinion for the Court by Justice Scalia, affirmed.

The position taken by the Court of Appeals goes too far. A judge can acquire a bias or prejudice from information obtained in judicial proceedings that make him or her unfit to sit further in the case. As to what constitutes a "bias or prejudice,"

> Not all unfavorable disposition towards an individual (or his case) is properly described by those terms. One would not say, for example, that world opinion is biased or prejudiced against Adolf Hitler. The words connote a favorable or unfavorable disposition or opinion that is somehow wrongful or inappropriate, either because it is undeserved, or because it rests upon knowledge that the subject ought not to possess (for example, a criminal juror who has been biased or prejudiced by receipt of inadmissible evidence concerning the defendant's prior criminal activities), or because it is excessive in degree (for example, a criminal juror who is so inflamed by properly admitted evidence of a defendant's prior criminal activities that he will vote guilty regardless of the facts).

___ U.S. at ___, 114 S.Ct. at 1155, 127 L.Ed.2d at ___. As applied to a judge,

> The judge who presides at a trial may, upon completion of the evidence, be exceedingly ill disposed towards the defendant, who has been shown to be a thoroughly reprehensible person. But the judge is not thereby recusable for bias or prejudice, since his knowledge and the opinion it produced were properly and necessarily acquired in the course of the proceedings, and are indeed sometimes (as in a bench trial) necessary to completion of the judge's task. As Judge Jerome Frank pithily put it: "Impartiality is not gullibility. Disinterestedness does not mean child-like innocence. If the judge did not form judgments of the actors in those court-house dramas called trials, he could never render decisions." * * * Also not subject to deprecatory characterization as "bias" or "prejudice" are opinions held by judges as a result of what they learned in earlier proceedings. It has long been regarded as normal and proper for a judge to sit in the same case upon its remand, and to sin in successive trials involving the same defendant.

___ U.S. at ___, 114 S.Ct. at 1155, 127 L.Ed.2d at ___. The reasons invoked by Petitioners—rulings and comments by the judge during the previous trial—are insufficient to require recusal under the statute: "All occurred in the course of judicial proceedings, and neither (1) relied upon knowledge acquired outside such proceedings nor (2) displayed deepseated and unequivocal antagonism that would render fair judgment impossible." ___ U.S. at ___, 114 S.Ct. at 1158, 127 L.Ed.2d at ___. Justice Kennedy, joined by Justices Blackmun, Stevens and Souter, concurred in the judgment and criticized the majority for requiring too great a showing of unfairness in order to mandate recusal.

Chapter 19

JOINDER AND SEVERANCE OF CHARGES AND DEFENDANTS

B. JOINDER AND SEVERANCE OF DEFENDANTS

Page 840. Add the following before Note 2:

1a. The Supreme Court considered the issue when severance of defendants is required because of mutually antagonistic defenses in Zafiro v. United States, ___ U.S. ___, 113 S.Ct. 933, 122 L.Ed.2d 317 (1993). Defendants Garcia and Soto were confronted by government agents while carrying a box up the stairs of an apartment building. They dropped the box and ran into an apartment. The box contained 55 pounds of cocaine. In the apartment, agents found two other persons, Zafiro and Martinez. A search of the apartment revealed a suitcase with 16 pounds of cocaine, a small quantity of heroin and 4 pounds of marijuana. Next to the suitcase was a sack containing over $20,000 in cash. All four were charged with various drug offenses. Each moved for severance from the other defendants. Soto claimed he knew nothing about what was in the box he and Garcia were carrying. Garcia claimed the box belonged to Soto and that Garcia was ignorant of its contents. Zafiro, whose apartment it was, claimed she knew nothing of the drugs in the suitcase, which belonged to her boyfriend, Martinez. Martinez' position was that he was just visiting his girlfriend and had no idea she was involved in distributing drugs. The District Court denied severance and a joint trial resulted in the conviction of each defendant. The Court of Appeals affirmed the convictions over the claim that severance was required because of the nature of the defenses presented at the trial.

The Supreme Court, in an opinion by Justice O'Connor, affirmed. Asserting there is a preference in the federal system for joint trials of defendants who are indicted together, the Court rejected the argument that severance is mandated whenever mutually antagonistic defenses are asserted. Rather,

> a district court should grant a severance under Rule 14 only if there is a serious risk that a joint trial would compromise a specific trial right of one of the defendants, or prevent the jury from making a reliable judgment about guilt or innocence. Such a risk might occur when evidence that the jury should not consider against a defendant and that would not be admissible if a defendant were tried alone is admitted against a codefendant. For example, evidence of a codefendant's wrongdoing in some circumstances erroneously could lead a jury to conclude that a defendant was guilty. When many defendants are tried together in a complex case and they have markedly different degrees of culpability, this risk of prejudice is heightened. Evidence that is probative of a defendant's guilt but technically admissible only against a codefendant also might present a risk of prejudice * * *. Conversely, a defendant might suffer prejudice if essential exculpatory evidence that would be available to a defendant tried alone were unavailable in a joint trial.

___ U.S. at ___, 113 S.Ct. at 938, 122 L.Ed.2d at 325. The Court concluded that the District Court's instructions to the jury to consider each defendant's fate individually were sufficient protection on these facts. Justice Stevens concurred in the judgment, noting that the defenses asserted in this case were not truly mutually antagonistic in that it was possible to believe one defense without also believing that the other defendant was for that reason guilty.

Chapter 20

DOUBLE JEOPARDY

A. FORMER ACQUITTAL

Page 860. Add the following after Note 5:

5a. The Supreme Court proposed an amendment in Federal Rules of Criminal Procedure Rule 29(b) to permit the trial judge to reserve ruling on a motion for judgment of acquittal made at the conclusion of the government's case. The trial court may rule after a verdict of guilty or after the jury is discharged without a verdict. In deciding a motion on which the trial judge has reserved ruling, the judge may consider only evidence that was admitted by the time the motion was made. The Advisory Committee Note states that an appellate court would be similarly limited in reviewing the correctness of the reserved ruling. The amendment became effective December 1, 1994.

Page 865. Add the following after Note 9:

9a. The petitioner in Schiro v. Farley, ___ U.S. ___, 114 S.Ct. 783, 127 L.Ed.2d 47 (1994) was charged in count one with knowingly killing another, in count two with killing another while committing rape and in count three with killing another while committing deviate conduct. The State sought the death penalty on counts two and three. The jury returned a verdict of guilty on count two and left the remaining verdict sheets blank. Under Indiana law, imposition of the death penalty requires the State to prove at the penalty phase of the proceedings the existence of at least one of nine aggravating circumstances, including that the defendant *intentionally* killed the victim while committing or attempting to commit rape. Although the jury recommended against the death penalty, the trial judge rejected that recommendation on the ground that the aggravating circumstance of intentional killing during rape had been shown. On direct appeals and in federal habeas, Petitioner unsuccessfully argued that the double jeopardy clause prohibited finding in the penalty phase that he had intentionally killed during rape because he had been acquitted of that theory by the jury in the guilt/innocence phase. He also argued the State was collaterally estopped from attempting to show intentional murder as an aggravating circumstance.

The Supreme Court, in an opinion authored by Justice O'Connor, affirmed denial of habeas relief. The Court rejected Petitioner's prior acquittal claim on the ground the guilt/innocence and penalty phases were part of a single trial. It distinguished *Bullington,*

> This case is manifestly different. Neither the prohibition against a successive trial on the issue of guilt, nor the *Bullington* prohibition against a second capital sentencing proceeding, is implicated here—the State did not reprosecute Schiro for intentional murder, nor did it force him to submit to a second death penalty hearing. It simply conducted a single sentencing hearing in the course of a single prosecution. The state is entitled to "one

> fair opportunity" to prosecute a defendant * * * and that opportunity extends not only to prosecution at the guilt phase, but also to present evidence at an ensuing sentencing proceeding.

___ U.S. at ___, 114 S.Ct. at 790, 127 L.Ed.2d at 58.

The Court refused to decide whether the constitutional principle of collateral estoppel (*Ashe v. Swenson,* Casebook p. 866) could apply to preclude a penalty phase verdict based upon a guilt/innocence phase finding. It concluded that Petitioner had failed to prove the threshold requirement that he had obtained a favorable finding from the jury at guilt innocence on the issue of intentional killing. The three counts were independent of each other; one was not a lesser included offense of another. The jury was not instructed to consider the counts in any particular order. The question of intent to kill was not disputed during the guilt/innocence phase.

B. MULTIPLE CONVICTIONS

Page 886. Add the following before Note 4:

3a. The double jeopardy implications of a drug possession tax was addressed in Department of Revenue of Montana v. Kurth Ranch, ___ U.S. ___, 114 S.Ct. 1937, 128 L.Ed.2d 767 (1994). Following a raid on the Kurth Ranch that resulted in seizure of marijuana plants and conviction of members of the Kurth family for conspiracy to possess marijuana, the State of Montana assessed a tax liability of almost $900,000 on the marijuana that was seized—approximately eight times the market value of the drugs seized. The Supreme Court, in an opinion by Justice Stevens, held that the imposition of the tax in this case violated the Double Jeopardy Clause. "As a general matter, the unlawfulness of an activity does not prevent its taxation * * *. Montana no doubt could collect its tax on the possession of marijuana, for example, if it had not previously punished the taxpayer for the same offense, or, indeed, if it had assessed the tax in the same proceeding that resulted in his conviction * * *. Here, we ask only whether the tax has punitive characteristics that subject it to the constraints of the Double Jeopardy Clause." ___ U.S. at ___, 114 S.Ct. at 1945, 128 L.Ed.2d at 778. Relevant to determining whether the tax is punitive is its rate, which is quite high, that the tax is conditioned on the commission of a crime that resulted in arrest, that while it purports to be a tax on property it operates only on contraband that has already presumably been destroyed by the authorities that seized it. The Court concluded that the Montana tax was punitive and that its imposition in proceedings that followed conviction for possession of the property taxed violated the Double Jeopardy Clause as interpreted in United States v. Halper.

Page 886. Add the following after Note 4:

5. Does the Double Jeopardy Clause prohibition against multiple punishments for the same offense prohibit prosecution for an offense the underlying conduct of which has already been taken into account under federal Sentencing Guidelines as "relevant conduct" in the sentence for a previous conviction? The petitioner in Witte v. United States, ___ U.S. ___, 115 S.Ct. 2199, ___ L.Ed.2d ___ (1995) was convicted of a marijuana offense. Conspiracy to commit a cocaine offense was taken into account as relevant conduct by the court in selecting the

sentence in the marijuana case. Later, petitioner was indicted for the cocaine offense and interposed a claim of double jeopardy. The District Court upheld the claim but the Fifth Circuit reversed. The Supreme Court, in an opinion by Justice O'Connor, affirmed. It held that consideration of the defendant character at sentencing, as evidenced in part by prior criminal conduct, is not punishment for that conduct but only for the offense for which he is being sentenced. Accordingly, as in the case of repeat offender statutes that enhance punishment for prior criminal convictions, multiple punishment for the same offense does not occur when unadjudicated criminal conduct is taken into account in sentencing for conviction of a different offense. The Sentencing Guidelines further protect against "double counting" by providing for concurrent sentences should the petitioner be found guilty of the cocaine charge, because it was previously taken into account as "relevant conduct" in the marijuana case.

Page 893. Add the following:

UNITED STATES v. DIXON

Supreme Court of the United States, 1993.
___ U.S. ___, 113 S.Ct. 2849, 125 L.Ed.2d 556.

JUSTICE SCALIA announced the judgment of the Court and delivered the opinion of the Court with respect to Parts I, II, and IV, and an opinion with respect to Parts III and V, in which JUSTICE KENNEDY joins.

In both of these cases, respondents were tried for criminal contempt of court for violating court orders that prohibited them from engaging in conduct that was later the subject of a criminal prosecution. We consider whether the subsequent criminal prosecutions are barred by the Double Jeopardy Clause.

I

Respondent Alvin Dixon was arrested for second-degree murder and was released on bond. Consistent with the District of Columbia's bail law authorizing the judicial officer to impose any condition that "will reasonably assure the appearance of the person for trial or the safety of any other person or the community," D.C.Code Ann. § 23–1321(a) (1989), Dixon's release form specified that he was not to commit "any criminal offense," and warned that any violation of the conditions of release would subject him "to revocation of release, an order of detention, and prosecution for contempt of court." See § 23–1329(a) (authorizing those sanctions).

While awaiting trial, Dixon was arrested and indicted for possession of cocaine with intent to distribute, in violation of D.C.Code Ann. § 33–541(a)(1) (1988). The court issued an order requiring Dixon to show cause why he should not be held in contempt or have the terms of his pretrial release modified. At the show-cause hearing, four police officers testified to facts surrounding the alleged drug offense; Dixon's counsel cross-examined these witnesses and introduced other evidence. The court concluded that the Government had established " 'beyond a reasonable doubt that [Dixon] was in possession of drugs and that those drugs were possessed with the intent to distribute.' " 598 A.2d 724, 728 (D.C.1991). The court therefore found Dixon guilty of criminal contempt under § 23–1329(c), which allows contempt sanctions after expedited proceedings without a jury and "in accordance with principles applicable to proceedings for criminal contempt." For his contempt, Dixon was sentenced to 180 days in jail. D.C.Code § 23–1329(c) (maximum penalty of six months' imprisonment and $1000 fine). He later moved to dismiss the cocaine indictment on double jeopardy grounds; the trial court granted the motion.

Respondent Michael Foster's route to this Court is similar. Based on Foster's alleged physical attacks upon her in the past, Foster's estranged wife Ana obtained a civil protection order (CPO) in Superior Court of the District of Columbia. See D.C.Code Ann. § 16–1005(c) (1989) (CPO may be issued upon a showing of good cause to believe that the subject "has committed or is threatening an intrafamily offense"). The order, to which Foster consented, required that he not " 'molest, assault, or in any manner threaten or physically abuse' " Ana Foster; a separate order, not implicated here, sought to protect her mother. 598 A.2d, at 725–726.

Over the course of eight months, Ana Foster filed three separate motions to have her husband held in contempt for numerous violations of the CPO. Of the 16 alleged episodes, the only charges relevant here are three separate instances of threats (on November 12, 1987, and March 26 and May 17, 1988) and two assaults (on November 6, 1987, and May 21, 1988), in the most serious of which Foster "threw [his wife] down basement stairs, kicking her body[,] ... pushed her head into the floor causing head injuries, [and Ana Foster] lost consciousness." 598 A.2d, at 726.

After issuing a notice of hearing and ordering Foster to appear, the court held a 3–day bench trial. Counsel for Ana Foster and her mother prosecuted the action; the United States was not represented at trial, although the United States Attorney was apparently aware of the action, as was the court aware of a separate grand jury proceeding on some of the alleged criminal conduct. As to the assault charges, the court stated that Ana Foster would have "to prove as an element, first that there was a Civil Protection Order, and then [that] ... the assault as defined by the criminal code, in fact occurred." At the close of the plaintiffs' case, the court granted Foster's motion for acquittal on various counts, including the alleged threats on November 12 and May 17. Foster then took the stand and generally denied the allegations. The court found Foster guilty beyond a reasonable doubt of four counts of criminal contempt (three violations of Ana Foster's CPO, and one violation of the CPO obtained by her mother), including the November 6, 1987 and May 21, 1988 assaults, but acquitted him on other counts, including the

March 26 alleged threats. He was sentenced to an aggregate 600 days' imprisonment. See § 16–1005(f) (authorizing contempt punishment); Sup.Ct. of D.C. Intrafamily Rules 7(c), 12(e) (maximum punishment of six months' imprisonment and $300 fine).

The United States Attorney's Office later obtained an indictment charging Foster with simple assault on or about November 6, 1987 (Count I, violation of § 22–504); threatening to injure another on or about November 12, 1987, and March 26 and May 17, 1988 (Counts II–IV, violation of § 22–2307); and assault with intent to kill on or about May 21, 1988 (Count V, violation of § 22–501). App. 43–44. Ana Foster was the complainant in all counts; the first and last counts were based on the events for which Foster had been held in contempt, and the other three were based on the alleged events for which Foster was acquitted of contempt. Like Dixon, Foster filed a motion to dismiss, claiming a double jeopardy bar to all counts, and also collateral estoppel as to Counts II–IV. The trial court denied the double-jeopardy claim and did not rule on the collateral-estoppel assertion.

The Government appealed the double jeopardy ruling in *Dixon,* and Foster appealed the trial court's denial of his motion. The District of Columbia Court of Appeals consolidated the two cases, reheard them en banc, and, relying on our recent decision in Grady v. Corbin, 495 U.S. 508 (1990), ruled that both subsequent prosecutions were barred by the Double Jeopardy Clause. 598 A.2d, at 725. In its petition for certiorari, the Government presented the sole question "[w]hether the Double Jeopardy Clause bars prosecution of a defendant on substantive criminal charges based upon the same conduct for which he previously has been held in criminal contempt of court." We granted certiorari, 503 U.S. ___ (1992).

II

To place these cases in context, one must understand that they are the consequence of an historically anomalous use of the contempt power. In both *Dixon* and *Foster,* a court issued an order directing a particular individual not to commit criminal offenses. (In Dixon's case, the court incorporated the entire criminal code; in Foster's case, the criminal offense of simple assault.) That could not have occurred at common law, or in the 19th–century American judicial system.

* * *

The Double Jeopardy Clause, whose application to this new context we are called upon to consider, provides that no person shall "be subject for the same offence to be twice put in jeopardy of life or limb." U.S. Const., Amdt. 5. This protection applies both to successive punishments and to successive prosecutions for the same criminal offense. See North Carolina v. Pearce, 395 U.S. 711 (1969). It is well established that criminal contempt, at least the sort enforced through nonsummary proceedings, is "a crime in the ordinary sense." *Bloom,* supra, at 201. Accord, New Orleans v. The Steamship Co., 20 Wall. 387, 392 (1874).

We have held that constitutional protections for criminal defendants other than the double jeopardy provision apply in nonsummary criminal contempt prosecutions just as they do in other criminal prosecutions. See, e.g., Gompers v. Bucks Stove & Range Co., 221 U.S. 418, 444 (1911) (presumption of innocence, proof beyond a reasonable doubt, and guarantee against self-incrimination); Cooke v. United States, 267 U.S. 517, 537 (1925) (notice of charges, assistance of counsel, and right to present a defense); In re Oliver, 333 U.S. 257, 278 (1948) (public trial). We think it obvious, and today hold, that the protection of the Double Jeopardy Clause likewise attaches. Accord, Menna v. New York, 423 U.S. 61 (1975) (*per curiam*); Colombo v. New York, 405 U.S. 9 (1972) (*per curiam*).

In both the multiple punishment and multiple prosecution contexts, this Court has concluded that where the two offenses for which the defendant is punished or tried cannot survive the "same-elements" test, the double jeopardy bar applies. See, e.g., Brown v. Ohio, 432 U.S. 161, 168–169 (1977); Blockburger v. United States, 284 U.S. 299, 304 (1932) (multiple punishment); Gavieres v. United States, 220 U.S. 338, 342 (1911) (successive prosecutions). The same-elements test, sometimes referred to as the "*Blockburger* " test, inquires whether each offense contains an element not contained in the other; if not, they are the "same offence" and double jeopardy bars additional punishment and successive prosecution. In a case such as *Yancy,* for example, in which the contempt prosecution was for disruption of judicial business, the same-elements test would not bar subsequent prosecution for the criminal assault that was part of the disruption, because the contempt offense did not require the element of criminal conduct, and the criminal offense did not require the element of disrupting judicial business.[1]

We recently held in *Grady* that in addition to passing the *Blockburger* test, a subsequent prosecution must satisfy a "same-conduct" test to avoid the double jeopardy bar. The *Grady* test provides that, "if, to establish an essential element of an offense charged in that prosecution, the government will prove conduct that constitutes an offense for which the defendant has already been prosecuted," a second prosecution may not be had.

III

A

The first question before us today is whether *Blockburger* analysis permits subsequent prosecution in this new criminal contempt context,

[1] State v. Yancy, 4 N.C. 133 (1814), it should be noted, involved what is today called summary contempt. We have not held, and do not mean by this example to decide, that the double-jeopardy guarantee applies to such proceedings.

where judicial order has prohibited criminal act. If it does, we must then proceed to consider whether *Grady* also permits it.

We begin with *Dixon*. The statute applicable in Dixon's contempt prosecution provides that "[a] person who has been conditionally released ... and who has violated a condition of release shall be subject to ... prosecution for contempt of court." § 23–1329(a). Obviously, Dixon could not commit an "offence" under this provision until an order setting out conditions was issued. The statute by itself imposes no legal obligation on anyone. Dixon's cocaine possession, although an offense under D.C.Code Ann. § 33–541(a) (1988 and Supp.1992), was not an offense under § 23–1329 until a judge incorporated the statutory drug offense into his release order.

In this situation, in which the contempt sanction is imposed for violating the order through commission of the incorporated drug offense, the later attempt to prosecute Dixon for the drug offense resembles the situation that produced our judgment of double jeopardy in Harris v. Oklahoma, 433 U.S. 682 (1977) (*per curiam*). There we held that a subsequent prosecution for robbery with a firearm was barred by the Double Jeopardy Clause, because the defendant had already been tried for felony-murder based on the same underlying felony. We have described our terse *per curiam* in *Harris* as standing for the proposition that, for double jeopardy purposes, "the crime generally described as felony murder" is not "a separate offense distinct from its various elements." Illinois v. Vitale, 447 U.S. 410, 420–421 (1980). Accord, Whalen v. United States, 445 U.S. 684, 694 (1980). So too here, the "crime" of violating a condition of release cannot be abstracted from the "element" of the violated condition. The *Dixon* court order incorporated the entire governing criminal code in the same manner as the *Harris* felony-murder statute incorporated the several enumerated felonies. Here, as in *Harris*, the underlying substantive criminal offense is "a species of lesser-included offense." *Vitale*, supra, at 420. Accord, *Whalen*, supra.

* * *

* * * Because Dixon's drug offense did not include any element not contained in his previous contempt offense, his subsequent prosecution violates the Double Jeopardy Clause.

The foregoing analysis obviously applies as well to Count I of the indictment against Foster, charging assault in violation of § 22–504, based on the same event that was the subject of his prior contempt conviction for violating the provision of the CPO forbidding him to commit simple assault under § 22–504. The subsequent prosecution for assault fails the *Blockburger* test, and is barred.

B

The remaining four counts in *Foster*, assault with intent to kill (Count V; § 22–501) and threats to injure or kidnap (Counts II–IV;

§ 22–2307), are not barred under *Blockburger.* As to Count V: Foster's conduct on May 21, 1988 was found to violate the Family Division's order that he not "molest, assault, or in any manner threaten or physically abuse" his wife. At the contempt hearing, the court stated that Ana Foster's attorney, who prosecuted the contempt, would have to prove first, knowledge of a CPO, and second, a willful violation of one of its conditions, here simple assault as defined by the criminal code. On the basis of the same episode, Foster was then indicted for violation of § 22–501, which proscribes assault with intent to kill. Under governing law, that offense requires proof of specific intent to kill; simple assault does not. See Logan v. United States, 483 A.2d 664, 672–673 (D.C. 1984). Similarly, the contempt offense required proof of knowledge of the CPO, which assault with intent to kill does not. Applying the *Blockburger* elements test, the result is clear: These crimes were different offenses and the subsequent prosecution did not violate the Double Jeopardy Clause.

Counts II, III, and IV of Foster's indictment are likewise not barred. These charged Foster under § 22–2307 (forbidding anyone to "threate[n] ... to kidnap any person or to injure the person of another or physically damage the property of any person") for his alleged threats on three separate dates. Foster's contempt prosecution included charges that, on the same dates, he violated the CPO provision ordering that he not "in any manner threaten" Ana Foster. Conviction of the contempt required willful violation of the CPO—which conviction under § 22–2307 did not; and conviction under § 22–2307 required that the threat be a threat to kidnap, to inflict bodily injury, or to damage property—which conviction of the contempt (for violating the CPO provision that Foster not "in any manner threaten") did not. Each offense therefore contained a separate element, and the *Blockburger* test for double jeopardy was not met.

IV

Having found that at least some of the counts at issue here are not barred by the *Blockburger* test, we must consider whether they are barred by the new, additional double jeopardy test we announced three Terms ago in *Grady v. Corbin.* They undoubtedly are, since *Grady* prohibits "a subsequent prosecution if, to establish an essential element of an offense charged in that prosecution [here, assault as an element of assault with intent to kill, or threatening as an element of threatening bodily injury], the government will prove conduct that constitutes an offense for which the defendant has already been prosecuted [here, the assault and the threatening, which conduct constituted the offense of violating the CPO]." 495 U.S., at 510.

We have concluded, however, that *Grady* must be overruled. Unlike *Blockburger* analysis, whose definition of what prevents two crimes from being the "same offence," U.S. Const., Amdt. 5, has deep historical roots and has been accepted in numerous precedents of this Court. *Grady* lacks constitutional roots. The "same-conduct" rule it announced is wholly inconsistent with earlier Supreme Court precedent and with the clear common-law understanding of double jeopardy. See, e.g., Gavieres v. United States, 220 U.S., at 345 (in subsequent prosecution, "[w]hile it is true that the conduct of the accused was one and the same, two offenses resulted, each of which had an element not embraced in the other"). We need not discuss the many proofs of these statements, which were set forth at length in the *Grady* dissent. See 495 U.S., at 526 (Scalia, J., dissenting).

* * *

But *Grady* was not only wrong in principle; it has already proved unstable in application. Less than two years after it came down, in United States v. Felix, 503 U.S. ___ (1992), we were forced to recognize a large exception to it. There we concluded that a subsequent prosecution for conspiracy to manufacture, possess, and distribute methamphetamine was not barred by a previous conviction for attempt to manufacture the same substance. We offered as a justification for avoiding a "literal" (i.e., faithful) reading of *Grady* "longstanding authority" to the effect that prosecution for conspiracy is not precluded by prior prosecution for the substantive offense. Of course the very existence of such a large and longstanding "exception" to the *Grady* rule gave cause for concern that the rule was not an accurate expression of the law. This "past practice" excuse is not available to support the ignoring of *Grady* in the present case, since there is no Supreme Court precedent even discussing this fairly new breed of successive prosecution (criminal contempt for violation of a court order prohibiting a crime, followed by prosecution for the crime itself).

A hypothetical based on the facts in *Harris* reinforces the conclusion that *Grady* is a continuing source of confusion and must be overruled. Suppose the State first tries the defendant for felony-murder, based on robbery, and then indicts the defendant for robbery with a firearm in the same incident. Absent *Grady,* our cases provide a clear answer to the double-jeopardy claim in this situation. Under *Blockburger,* the second prosecution is not barred—as it clearly was not barred at common law, as a famous case establishes. In King v. Vandercomb, 2 Leach. 708, 717, 168 Eng.Rep. 455, 460 (K.B.1796), the government abandoned, midtrial, prosecution of defendant for burglary by breaking and entering and stealing goods, because it turned out that no property had been removed on the date of the alleged burglary. The defendant was then prosecuted for burglary by breaking and entering with intent to steal. That second prosecution was allowed, because "these two offences are so distinct in their nature, that evidence of one of them will not support an indictment for the other." Ibid. Accord, English and American cases cited in *Grady,* 495 U.S., at 532–535 (Scalia, J., dissenting).

Having encountered today yet another situation in which the pre-*Grady* understanding of the Double Jeopardy Clause allows a second trial, though the "same-conduct" test would not, we think it time to acknowledge what is now, three years after *Grady,* compellingly clear: the case was a mistake. We do not lightly reconsider a precedent, but, because *Grady* contradicted an "unbroken line of decisions," contained "less than accurate" historical analysis, and has produced "confusion," we do so here. Solorio v. United States, 483 U.S. 435, 439, 442, 450 (1987). Although *stare decisis* is the "preferred course" in constitutional adjudication, "when governing decisions are unworkable or are badly reasoned, 'this Court has never felt constrained to follow precedent.'" Payne v. Tennessee, 501 U.S. ___, ___ (1991) (quoting Smith v. Allwright, 321 U.S. 649, 665 (1944), and collecting examples). We would mock *stare decisis* and only add chaos to our double jeopardy jurisprudence by pretending that *Grady* survives when it does not. We therefore accept the Government's invitation to overrule *Grady,* and Counts II, III, IV, and V of Foster's subsequent prosecution are not barred.[17]

V

Dixon's subsequent prosecution, as well as Count I of Foster's subsequent prosecution, violate the Double Jeopardy Clause.[18] For the reasons set forth in Part IV, the other Counts of Foster's subsequent prosecution do not violate the Double Jeopardy Clause.[19] The judgment of the District of Columbia Court of Appeals is affirmed in part and reversed in part, and the case is remanded for proceedings not inconsistent with this opinion.

It is so ordered.

CHIEF JUSTICE REHNQUIST, with whom JUSTICE O'CONNOR and JUSTICE THOMAS join, concurring in part and dissenting in part.

Respondent Alvin Dixon possessed cocaine with intent to distribute it. For that he was held in contempt of court for violating a condition of his bail release. He was later criminally charged for the same conduct with possession with intent to distribute cocaine. Respondent Michael Foster assaulted and threatened his estranged wife. For that he was held in contempt of court for violating a civil protection order entered in a domestic relations proceeding. He was later criminally charged for the same conduct with assault, threatening to injure another, and assault with intent to kill.

The Court today concludes that the Double Jeopardy Clause prohibits the subsequent prosecutions of Foster for assault and Dixon for

[17] We do not address the motion to dismiss the threat counts based on collateral estoppel, see *Ashe v. Swenson,* supra, because neither lower court ruled on that issue.

[18] Justices White, Stevens, and Souter concur in this portion of the judgment.

[19] Justice Blackmun concurs only in the judgment with respect to this portion.

possession with intent to distribute cocaine, but does not prohibit the subsequent prosecutions of Foster for threatening to injure another or for assault with intent to kill. After finding that at least some of the charges here are not prohibited by the "same-elements" test set out in Blockburger v. United States, 284 U.S. 299, 304 (1932), the Court goes on to consider whether there is a double-jeopardy bar under the "same-conduct" test set out in Grady v. Corbin, 495 U.S. 508, 510 (1990), and determines that there is. However, because the same-conduct test is inconsistent with the text and history of the Double Jeopardy Clause, was a departure from our earlier precedents, and has proven difficult to apply, the Court concludes that *Grady* must be overruled. I do not join Part III of Justice Scalia's opinion because I think that none of the criminal prosecutions in this case were barred under *Blockburger*. I must then confront the expanded version of double jeopardy embodied in *Grady*. For the reasons set forth in the *Grady* dissent, supra, at 526 (Scalia, J., dissenting), and in Part IV of the Court's opinion, I, too, think that *Grady* must be overruled. I therefore join Parts I, II, and IV of the Court's opinion, and write separately to express my disagreement with Justice Scalia's application of *Blockburger* in Part III.

In my view, *Blockburger*'s same-elements test requires us to focus not on the terms of the particular court orders involved, but on the elements of contempt of court in the ordinary sense. Relying on Harris v. Oklahoma, 433 U.S. 682 (1977), a three-paragraph *per curiam* in an unargued case, Justice Scalia concludes otherwise today, and thus incorrectly finds in Part III–A of his opinion that the subsequent prosecutions of Dixon for drug distribution and of Foster for assault violated the Double Jeopardy Clause. In so doing, Justice Scalia rejects the traditional view—shared by every federal court of appeals and state supreme court that addressed the issue prior to *Grady*—that, as a general matter, double jeopardy does not bar a subsequent prosecution based on conduct for which a defendant has been held in criminal contempt. I cannot subscribe to a reading of *Harris* that upsets this previously well-settled principle of law. Because the generic crime of contempt of court has different elements than the substantive criminal charges in this case, I believe that they are separate offenses under *Blockburger*. I would therefore limit *Harris* to the context in which it arose: where the crimes in question are analogous to greater and lesser included offenses. The crimes at issue here bear no such resemblance.

* * *

In sum, I think that the substantive criminal prosecutions in this case, which followed convictions for criminal contempt, did not violate the Double Jeopardy Clause, at least before our decision in *Grady*. Under *Grady*, "the Double Jeopardy Clause bars a subsequent prosecution if, to establish an essential element of an offense charged in that prosecution, the government will prove conduct that constitutes an offense for which the defendant has already been prosecuted." 495 U.S., at 510. As the Court points out, this case undoubtedly falls within that expansive formulation: To secure convictions on the substantive criminal charges in this case, the Government will have to prove conduct that was the basis for the contempt convictions. Forced, then, to confront *Grady,* I join the Court in overruling that decision.

JUSTICE WHITE, with whom JUSTICE STEVENS joins, and with whom JUSTICE SOUTER joins as to Part I, concurring in the judgment in part and dissenting in part.

I am convinced that the Double Jeopardy Clause bars prosecution for an offense if the defendant already has been held in contempt for its commission. Therefore, I agree with the Court's conclusion that both Dixon's prosecution for possession with intent to distribute cocaine and Foster's prosecution for simple assault were prohibited. In my view, however, Justice Scalia's opinion gives short shrift to the arguments raised by the United States. I also am uncomfortable with the reasoning underlying this holding, in particular the application of Blockburger v. United States, 284 U.S. 299 (1932), to the facts of this case, a reasoning that betrays an overly technical interpretation of the Constitution. As a result, I concur only in the judgment in Part III–A.

The mischief in Justice Scalia's approach is far more apparent in the second portion of today's decision. Constrained by his narrow reading of the Double Jeopardy Clause, he asserts that the fate of Foster's remaining counts depends on Grady v. Corbin, 495 U.S. 508 (1990), which the Court then chooses to overrule. I do not agree. Resolution of the question presented by Foster's case no more requires reliance on *Grady* than it points to reasons for reversing that decision. Rather, as I construe the Clause, double jeopardy principles compel equal treatment of *all* of Foster's counts. I dissent from the Court's holding to the contrary. Inasmuch as *Grady* has been dragged into this case, however, I agree with Justice Blackmun and Justice Souter that it should not be overruled. From this aspect of the Court's opinion as well, I dissent.

* * *

II

If, as the Court agrees, the Double Jeopardy Clause cannot be ignored in this context, my view is that the subsequent prosecutions in both *Dixon* and *Foster* were impermissible as to *all* counts. I reach this conclusion because the offenses at issue in the contempt proceedings were either identical to, or lesser included offenses of, those charged in the subsequent prosecutions. Justice Scalia's contrary conclusion as to some of Foster's counts, which he reaches by exclusive focus on the formal elements of the relevant crimes, is divorced from the purposes of the constitutional provision he purports to apply. Moreover, the results to which this approach would lead are indefensible.

A

The contempt orders in *Foster* and *Dixon* referred in one case to the District's laws regarding assaults and threats, and, in the other, to the criminal code in its entirety. The prohibitions imposed by the court orders, in other words, duplicated those already in place by virtue of the criminal statutes. Aside from differences in the sanctions inflicted, the distinction between being punished for violation of the criminal laws and being punished for violation of the court orders, therefore, is simply this: Whereas in the former case "the entire population" is subject to prosecution, in the latter such authority extends only to "those particular persons whose legal obligations result from their earlier participation in proceedings before the court." *Young,* 481 U.S., at 800, n. 10. But the *offenses* that are to be sanctioned in either proceeding must be similar, since the contempt orders incorporated, in full or in part, the criminal code.

Thus, in this case, the offense for which Dixon was held in contempt was possession with intent to distribute drugs. Since he previously had been indicted for precisely the same offense, the double jeopardy bar should apply. In Foster's contempt proceeding, he was acquitted with respect to threats allegedly made on November 12, 1987, and March 26 and May 17, 1988. He was found in contempt of court for having committed the following offenses: Assaulting his wife on November 6, 1987, and May 21, 1988, and threatening her on September 17, 1987. 598 A.2d, at 727; App. 42. The subsequent indictment charged Foster with simple assault on November 6, 1987 (Count I); threatening to injure another on or about November 12, 1987, and March 26 and May 17, 1988 (Counts II, III, and IV); and assault with intent to kill on or about May 21, 1988 (Count V). All of the offenses for which Foster was either convicted or acquitted in the contempt proceeding were similar to, or lesser included offenses of, those charged in the subsequent indictment. Because "the Fifth Amendment forbids successive prosecution ... for a greater and lesser included offense," Brown v. Ohio, 432 U.S. 161, 169 (1977); see also *Grafton,* 206 U.S., at 349–351, the second set of trials should be barred in their entirety.

B

Professing strict adherence to *Blockburger's* so-called "same elements" test, see *Blockburger v. United States,* 284 U.S. 299 (1932), Justice Scalia opts for a more circuitous approach. The elements of the crime of contempt, he reasons, in this instance are (1) the existence and knowledge of a court, or CPO; and (2) commission of the underlying substantive offense. Where the criminal conduct that forms the basis of the contempt order is identical to that charged in the subsequent trial, Justice Scalia concludes, *Blockburger* forbids retrial. All elements of Foster's simple assault offense being included in his previous contempt offense, prosecution on that ground is precluded. The same is true of

Dixon's drug offense. I agree with this conclusion, though would reach it rather differently: Because in a successive prosecution case the risk is that a person will have to defend himself more than once against the same charge, I would have put to the side the CPO (which, as it were, triggered the court's authority to punish the defendant for acts already punishable under the criminal laws) and compared the substantive offenses of which respondents stood accused in both prosecutions.

The significance of our disaccord is far more manifest where an element is added to the second prosecution. Under Justice Scalia's view, the double jeopardy barrier is then removed because each offense demands proof of an element the other does not: Foster's conviction for contempt requires proof of the existence and knowledge of a CPO, which conviction for assault with intent to kill does not; his conviction for assault with intent to kill requires proof of an intent to kill, which the contempt conviction did not. Finally, though he was acquitted in the contempt proceedings with respect to the alleged November 12, March 26, and May 17 threats, his conviction under the threat charge in the subsequent trial required the additional proof that the threat be to kidnap, to inflict bodily injury, or to damage property. As to these counts, and absent any collateral estoppel problem, Justice Scalia finds that the Constitution does not prohibit retrial.

The distinction drawn by Justice Scalia is predicated on a reading of the Double Jeopardy Clause that is abstracted from the purposes the constitutional provision is designed to promote. To focus on the statutory elements of a crime makes sense where *cumulative* punishment is at stake, for there the aim simply is to uncover legislative intent. The *Blockburger* inquiry, accordingly, serves as a means to determine this intent, as our cases have recognized. See Missouri v. Hunter, 459 U.S., at 368. But, as Justice Souter shows, adherence to legislative will has very little to do with the important interests advanced by double jeopardy safeguards against *successive* prosecutions. The central purpose of the Double Jeopardy Clause being to protect against vexatious multiple prosecutions, see *Hunter,* supra, at 365; United States v. Wilson, 420 U.S., at 343, these interests go well beyond the prevention of unauthorized punishment. The same-elements test is an inadequate safeguard, for it leaves the constitutional guarantee at the mercy of a legislature's decision to modify statutory definitions. Significantly, therefore, this Court has applied an inflexible version of the same-elements test only once, in 1911, in a successive prosecution case, see Gavieres v. United States, 220 U.S. 338 (1911), and has since noted that "[t]he *Blockburger* test is not the only standard for determining whether successive prosecutions impermissibly involve the same offense." *Brown,* 432 U.S., at 166–167, n. 6. Rather, "[e]ven if two offenses are sufficiently different to permit the imposition of consecutive sentences, successive prosecutions will be barred in some circumstances where the second prosecution requires the relitigation of factual issues already resolved by the first." Ibid.

Take the example of Count V in *Foster:* For all intents and purposes, the offense for which he was convicted in the contempt proceeding was his assault against his wife. The majority, its eyes fixed on the rigid elements-test, would have his fate turn on whether his subsequent prosecution charges "simple assault" or "assault with intent to kill." Yet, because the crime of "simple assault" is included within the crime of "assault with intent to kill," the reasons that bar retrial under the first hypothesis are equally present under the second: These include principles of finality, see *United States v. Wilson,* supra, at 343; protecting Foster from "embarrassment" and "expense," Green v. United States, 355 U.S., at 187; and preventing the government from gradually fine-tuning its strategy, thereby minimizing exposure to a mistaken conviction. Id., at 188. See also Tibbs v. Florida, 457 U.S. 31, 41 (1982); Arizona v. Washington, 434 U.S. 497, 503–504 (1978); supra, at 5.

Analysis of the threat charges (Counts II–IV) makes the point more clearly still. In the contempt proceeding, it will be recalled, Foster was acquitted of the—arguably lesser-included—offense of threatening "in any manner." As we have stated,

> "the law attaches particular significance to an acquittal. To permit a second trial after an acquittal, however mistaken the acquittal might have been, would present an unacceptably high risk that the Government, with its vastly superior resources, might wear down the defendant so that 'even though innocent he may be found guilty.'" United States v. Scott, 437 U.S. 82, 91 (1978) (citation omitted).

To allow the government to proceed on the threat counts would present precisely the risk of erroneous conviction the Clause seeks to avoid. That the prosecution had to establish the existence of the CPO in the first trial, in short, does not in any way modify the prejudice potentially caused to a defendant by consecutive trials.

To respond, as the majority appears to do, that concerns relating to the defendant's interests against repeat trials are "unjustified" because prosecutors "have little to gain and much to lose" from bringing successive prosecutions and because "the Government must be deterred from abusive, repeated prosecutions of a single offender for similar offenses by the sheer press of other demands upon prosecutorial and judicial resources," ante, at 21–22, n. 15, is to get things exactly backwards. The majority's prophesies might be correct, and double jeopardy might be a problem that will simply take care of itself. Not so, however, according to the Constitution, whose firm prohibition against double jeopardy cannot be satisfied by wishful thinking.

C

* * *

III

Once it is agreed that the Double Jeopardy Clause applies in this context, the Clause, properly construed, both governs this case and disposes of the distinction between Foster's charges upon which Justice Scalia relies. I therefore see little need to draw *Grady* into this dispute. In any event, the United States itself has not attempted to distinguish between *Dixon* and *Foster* or between the charges of "assault" on the one hand and, on the other, "assault with intent to kill" and "threat to injure another." The issue was not raised before the Court of Appeals or considered by it, and it was neither presented in the petition for certiorari nor briefed by either party. Under these circumstances, it is injudicious to address this matter. See, e.g., Mazer v. Stein, 347 U.S. 201, 206, n. 5 (1954); Adickes v. S.H. Kress & Co., 398 U.S. 144, 147, n. 2 (1970).

The majority nonetheless has chosen to consider *Grady* anew and to overrule it. I agree with Justice Blackmun and Justice Souter that such a course is both unwarranted and unwise. Hence, I dissent from the judgment overruling *Grady.*

IV

Believing that the Double Jeopardy Clause bars Foster's and Dixon's successive prosecutions on all counts, I would affirm the judgment of the District of Columbia Court of Appeals. I concur in the judgment of the Court in Part III–A which holds that Dixon's subsequent prosecution and Count I of Foster's subsequent prosecution were barred. I disagree with Justice Scalia's application of *Blockburger* in Part III–B. From Part IV of the opinion, in which the majority decides to overrule *Grady,* I dissent.

JUSTICE BLACKMUN, concurring in the judgment in part and dissenting in part.

I cannot agree that contempt of court is the "same offence" under the Double Jeopardy Clause as either assault with intent to kill or possession of cocaine with intent to distribute it. I write separately to emphasize two interrelated points.

I

I agree with Justice Souter that "the *Blockburger* test is not the exclusive standard for determining whether the rule against successive prosecutions applies in a given case." I also share both his and Justice White's dismay that the Court so cavalierly has overruled a precedent that is barely three years old and that has proved neither unworkable nor unsound. I continue to believe that Grady v. Corbin, 495 U.S. 508 (1990), was correctly decided, and that the Double Jeopardy Clause prohibits a subsequent criminal prosecution where the proof required to convict on the later offense would require proving conduct that constitutes an offense for which a defendant already has been prosecuted.

* * *

II

Contempt is one of the very few mechanisms available to a trial court to vindicate the authority of its orders. I fear that the Court's willingness to overlook the unique interests served by contempt proceedings not only will jeopardize the ability of trial courts to control those defendants under their supervision but will undermine their ability to respond effectively to unmistakable threats to their own authority and to those who have sought the court's protection.

This fact is poignantly stressed by the *amici:*

> "[C]ontempt litigators and criminal prosecutors seek to further different interests. A battered woman seeks to enforce her private order to end the violence against her. In contrast, the criminal prosecutor is vindicating *society's* interest in enforcing its criminal law. The two interests are not the same, and to consider the contempt litigator and the criminal prosecutor as one and the same would be to adopt an absurd fiction" (emphasis in original). Brief for Ayuda et al. as *Amici Curiae* 20.

Finally, I cannot so easily distinguish between "summary" and "nonsummary" contempt proceedings, for the interests served in both are fundamentally similar. It is as much a "disruption of judicial process" to disobey a judge's conditional release order as it is to disturb a judge's courtroom. And the interests served in vindicating the authority of the court are fundamentally different from those served by the prosecution of violations of the substantive criminal law. Because I believe that neither Dixon nor Foster would be "subject for the same offence to be twice put in jeopardy of life or limb," U.S. Const., Amdt. 5, I would reverse the judgment of the District of Columbia Court of Appeals.

JUSTICE SOUTER, with whom JUSTICE STEVENS joins, concurring in the judgment in part and dissenting in part.

While I agree with the Court as far as it goes in holding that a citation for criminal contempt and an indictment for violating a substantive criminal statute may amount to charges of the "same offence" for purposes of the Double Jeopardy Clause, U.S. Const., Amdt. 5, I cannot join the Court in restricting the Clause's reach and dismembering the protection against successive prosecution that the Constitution was meant to provide. The Court has read our precedents so narrowly as to leave them bereft of the principles animating that protection, and has chosen to overrule the most recent of the relevant cases, Grady v. Corbin, 495 U.S. 508 (1990), decided three years ago. Because I think that *Grady* was correctly decided, amounting merely to an expression of just those animating principles, and because, even if the decision had been wrong in the first instance, there is no warrant for overruling it now, I respectfully dissent. I join Part I of Justice White's opinion, and I would hold, as he would, both the prosecution of Dixon and the prosecution of Foster under all the counts of the indictment against him to be barred by the Double Jeopardy Clause.

* * *

VIII

Grady simply applied a rule with roots in our cases going back well over 100 years. *Nielsen* held that the Double Jeopardy Clause bars successive prosecutions for more than one statutory offense where the charges comprise the same act, and *Harris,* as understood in *Vitale,* is properly read as standing for the same rule. Overruling *Grady* alone cannot remove this principle from our constitutional jurisprudence. Only by uprooting the entire sequence of cases, *Grady, Vitale, Harris,* and *Nielsen,* could this constitutional principle be undone. Because I would not do that, I would affirm the judgment of the Court of Appeals. I concur in the judgment of the Court in *Dixon* and with respect to Count I in *Foster,* but respectfully dissent from the disposition of the case with respect to Counts II–V in *Foster.*

C. TERMINATION WITHOUT ACQUITTAL OR CONVICTION

1. MISTRIALS

Page 902. Insert the following new note into the Notes after Illinois v. Somerville:

5. In 1993, the Supreme Court added the following new rule to the Federal Rules of Criminal Procedure:

Rule 26.3 Mistrial

> Before ordering a mistrial, the court shall provide an opportunity for the government and for each defendant to comment on the propriety of the order, including whether each party consents or objects to a mistrial, and to suggest any alternatives.

The Advisory Committee explained that the rule was in part a response to several recent appellate decisions barring retrial of defendants after mistrials found on appeal to have been the result of precipitous action by district judges, who had failed to solicit the view of the parties as to the need for a mistrial and feasibility of any alternative action. The Committee added:

> The Committee regards the Rule as a balanced and modest procedural device which could benefit both the prosecution and the defense. * * * The

> Rule * * * ensures that the defendant has the opportunity to dissuade a judge from declaring a mistrial in a case where granting one would not be an abuse of discretion, but the defendant believes the prospects for a favorable outcome before that particular court or jury are stronger than they would be at a retrial.

Preliminary Draft of Proposed Amendments, Committee Note to Proposed Rule 26.3, 137 F.R.D. 417, 497 (1991).

Chapter 22

ADJUDICATION OF GUILT BY PLEA

A. ENTRY OF THE PLEA OF GUILTY

Page 935. Add the following before Note 2:

1a. The respondent in Parke v. Raley, ___ U.S. ___, 113 S.Ct. 517, 121 L.Ed.2d 391 (1992) challenged the admissibility of prior convictions under a Kentucky recidivist statute on the ground that the record in the prior cases did not show the waivers of constitutional rights required to be shown by *Boykin.* No stenographic record existed of the pleas of guilty upon which the convictions were based. The Sixth Circuit held, on federal habeas, that when no record exists the burden is upon the State to prove the validity of the plea and no presumption of regularity attaches to the judgment. It also held that the State must make that showing by clear and convincing evidence. The Supreme Court, in an opinion by Justice O'Connor, reversed. The Court noted that with respect to convictions that are several years old, a missing or nonexistent record is "not atypical." Without evidence that governmental misconduct is responsible for the absence of a record, the state is permitted to presume that a conviction was obtained in compliance with *Boykin* based upon a judgment of conviction. Therefore, the burden of producing evidence as to noncompliance with *Boykin* may constitutionally be placed upon the criminal defendant. This is fair since often the criminal defendant has the best access to information concerning the circumstances of the acceptance of the plea. The Court also held that if the state is given the burden of persuasion as to compliance with *Boykin,* the Due Process Clause does not require a higher standard of persuasion than a preponderance of the evidence. Justice Blackmun concurred in the judgment on the understanding that the Kentucky statutory scheme was a sentencing provision only and did not create a separate criminal offense.

C. PLEA BARGAINING

4. THE NECESSITY OF RESPECTING A BARGAIN ONCE MADE

Page 993. Add the following after Note 5:

5a. Federal Rules of Criminal Procedure 11(e)(6) provides that evidence of "any statement made in the course of plea discussions with an attorney for the government which do not result in a plea of guilty" are inadmissible in evidence. See Casebook p. 931. Can the defendant agree with the prosecutor to waive that exclusion as to statements that might be used to impeach later testimony in the event of a trial?

The respondent in United States v. Mezzanatto, ___ U.S. ___, 115 S.Ct. 797, 130 L.Ed.2d 697 (1995) made incriminatory statements during plea discussions with a prosecutor concerning his role in a drug distribution scheme. Before discussions began, he agreed to waive the protections of Rule 11(e) as to any statements he might make that could be used to impeach contradictory trial testimony. Plea discussions concluded without an agreement and the case went to trial. The government was permitted to impeach respondent's trial testimony with prior inconsistent statements he had made during the aborted plea discussions. The Ninth Circuit, viewing the exclusion as non-waivable, reversed the conviction. The Supreme Court, in an opinion by Justice Thomas, reversed the Ninth Circuit and reinstated the conviction.

The Court found nothing in the Rule to rebut the general presumption that legal rights can be waived by their intended beneficiary. Accordingly, it announced the rule that "absent some affirmative indication that the agreement was entered into unknowingly or involuntarily, an agreement to waive the exclusionary provisions of the plea-statement Rules is valid and enforceable." ___ U.S. at ___, 115 S.Ct. at 806, 130 L.Ed.2d at 710.

Justice Ginsburg concurred with the observation that an agreement to permit statements made during plea discussions to be admitted during the Government's case-in-chief might be dealt with differently on the ground admission would be inconsistent with Congress's intent to promote plea bargaining by the exclusionary provision.

Chapter 23

ADJUDICATION OF GUILT OR INNOCENCE BY TRIAL

A. PROOF BEYOND A REASONABLE DOUBT

Page 1009. Add the following to Note 4:

The Court further discussed harmless error in the context of burden-shifting jury instructions in Yates v. Evatt, 500 U.S. 391, 111 S.Ct. 1884, 114 L.Ed.2d 432 (1991). In Yates' murder trial, the court instructed the jury on the definition of murder, which included "malice" as an element. It further instructed the jury that malice is implied or presumed (1) from the willful, deliberate and intentional doing of an unlawful act and (2) from the use of a deadly weapon. The state supreme court found that these were mandatory presumptions, although rebuttable ones, and were, therefore, unconstitutional under *Sandstrom* and *Francis*. However, it found them to be harmless errors. The Supreme Court, in an opinion by Justice Souter, reversed. It established an approach to analyzing whether burden-shifting instructions were harmless under Chapman v. California (Casebook p. 1236) test of whether it appears "beyond a reasonable doubt that the error complained of did not contribute to the verdict obtained." The ultimate question is whether the "error [was] unimportant in relation to everything else the jury considered on the issue in question, as revealed by the record." The first step is to ask what evidence, based on the instructions and the record, the jury must have considered in reaching its verdict. The second step is to weigh the probative force of that evidence against the probative force of the invalid presumption. The standard is

> whether the force of the evidence presumably considered by the jury in accordance with the instructions is so overwhelming as to leave it beyond a reasonable doubt that the verdict resting on that evidence would have been the same in the absence of the presumption. It is only when the effect of the presumption is comparatively minimal to this degree that it can be said, in *Chapman's* words, that the presumption did not contribute to the verdict rendered.

500 U.S. at 405, 111 S.Ct. at 1893–94, 114 L.Ed.2d at 449. It then analyzed the evidence in light of that standard and concluded it could not find the errors harmless.

Page 1010. Add the following after Note 5:

5a. Trial courts sometimes attempt to define reasonable doubt in jury instructions mandating use of the constitutional standard of proof beyond a reasonable doubt. In Cage v. Louisiana, 498 U.S. 39, 111 S.Ct. 328, 112 L.Ed.2d 339 (1990), the trial court had included the following in the jury instructions concerning the meaning of reasonable doubt:

> This doubt, however, must be a reasonable one; that is one that is founded upon a real tangible substantial basis and not upon mere caprice and conjecture. *It must be such doubt as would give rise to a grave uncertainty,* raised in your mind by reasons on the unsatisfactory character of the evidence or lack thereof. A reasonable doubt is not a mere possible doubt. *It is an actual substantial doubt.* It is a doubt that a reasonable man can seriously entertain. What is required is not an absolute or mathematical certainty, but a *moral certainty.*

498 U.S. at 40, 111 S.Ct. at 329, 112 L.Ed.2d at 342 (emphasis in original). The Supreme Court, per curiam, found this instruction violated In re Winship,

> The charge * * * equated a reasonable doubt with a "grave uncertainty" and an "actual substantial doubt," and stated that what was required was a "moral certainty" that the defendant was guilty. It is plain to us that the words "substantial" and "grave," as they are commonly understood, suggest a higher degree of doubt than is required for acquittal under the reasonable doubt standard. When those statements are then considered with the reference to "moral certainty," rather than evidentiary certainty, it becomes clear that a reasonable juror could have interpreted the instruction to allow a finding of guilt based on a degree of proof below that required by the Due Process Clause.

498 U.S. at 41, 111 S.Ct. at 329–30, 112 L.Ed.2d at 342. What definition of reasonable doubt could a trial court give that would satisfy Due Process? Should a trial court refrain from giving the jury any definition at all? Is the trial court constitutionally required to give a definition? Is "proof beyond a reasonable doubt" a concept the jury can be expected to understand without elaboration?

The Court in Victor v. Nebraska, ___ U.S. ___, 114 S.Ct. 1239, 127 L.Ed.2d 583 (1994), in an opinion by Justice O'Connor, held that the instructions in that case and in Sandoval v. California did not violate due process. The instruction in Sandoval v. California defined reasonable doubt by using the words "moral evidence" and "moral certainty." Victor challenged the instruction in his case for using the terms "substantial doubt" and "strong probabilities" in defining the burden of proof. Unlike in Cage v. Louisiana, the Court concluded here that " 'taken as a whole, the instructions correctly conveyed the concept of reasonable doubt to the jury.' * * * There is no reasonable likelihood that the jurors who determined petitioners' guilt applied the instructions in a way that violated the Constitution." ___ U.S. at ___, 114 S.Ct. at 1251, 127 L.Ed.2d at 601.

A jury instruction on reasonable doubt that violates *Cage* cannot be harmless error, the Court held in Sullivan v. Louisana, ___ U.S. ___, 113 S.Ct. 2078, 124 L.Ed.2d 182 (1993). The Fifth Amendment requirement of proof beyond a reasonable doubt and the Sixth Amendment requirement of a jury verdict are interrelated, Justice Scalia reasoned for the Court, and a verdict returned by a jury inaccurately instructed on reasonable doubt does not meet the Sixth Amendment jury trial requirement. As applied to harmless error situations, the Sixth Amendment jury trial guarantee demands that a reviewing court inquire as to what if any effect the error had upon the verdict actually returned in the case. It does not permit an inquiry into what effect the error might have upon some "reasonable" jury. If under *Cage* a jury has been misinstructed on the prosecution's burden of proof, all of the jury's findings are vitiated. There is, therefore, no verdict to use in a harmless error analysis.

> There being no jury verdict of guilty-beyond-a-reasonable-doubt, the question whether the *same* verdict of guilty-beyond-a-reasonable-doubt would have been rendered absent the constitutional error is utterly meaningless. There is no *object,* so to speak, upon which harmless-error scrutiny can operate. The most an appellate court can conclude is that a jury *would surely have found* [the defendant] guilty beyond a reasonable doubt—not that the jury's actual finding of guilty beyond a reasonable doubt *would surely not have been different* absent the constitutional error. That is not enough.

___ U.S. at ___, 113 S.Ct. at 2082, 124 L.Ed.2d at 189–90 (emphasis in original). Alternatively, the Court reasoned, the right to a jury verdict of guilty beyond a reasonable doubt is "a 'basic protectio[n]' whose precise effects are unreasurable." Therefore, an instruction that violates this right is one of the "structural defects in the constitution of the trial mechanism, which defy analysis by 'harmless error' standards." Under Arizona v. Fulminante, ___ U.S. ___, 111 S.Ct. 1246, 113 L.Ed.2d. 302 (1991), such defects cannot be harmless error.

B. RIGHT TO TRIAL BY JURY

Page 1011. Add the following to the introductory note:

The Sixth Amendment right to jury trial and the Fifth Amendment right to proof beyond a reasonable doubt are "interrelated." Sullivan v. Louisiana, ___ U.S. ___, 113 S.Ct. 2078, 2081, 124 L.Ed.2d 182, ___ (1993). Together, "these provisions require criminal convictions to rest upon a jury determination that the defendant is guilty of every element of the crime with which he is charged, beyond a reasonable doubt." United States v. Gaudin, ___ U.S. ___, ___, 115 S.Ct. ___, ___, ___ L.Ed.2d ___, ___, 1995 WL 360212 (1995). *Gaudin* presented the question whether there is an exception to this general rule for the materiality of the allegedly false statement in a perjury prosecution. At Gaudin's trial for making false statements on federal loan documents, the trial judge instructed the jury that the Government was required to prove that the alleged false statements were material but he added:

> [t]he issue of materiality ... is not submitted to you for your decision but rather is a matter for the decision of the court. You are instructed that the statements charged in the indictment are material statements.

Finding that this was error, the Court considered and rejected the Government's contention that case law indicating that materiality is a matter for the court rather than the jury created or reflected an exception to the general Fifth and Sixth Amendment rule:

> [W]e find nothing like a consistent historical tradition supporting the proposition that the element of materiality in perjury prosecutions is to be decided by the judge. Since that proposition is contrary to the uniform general understanding (and we think the only understanding consistent with principle) that the Fifth and Sixth Amendments require conviction by a jury of all elements of

> the crime, we must reject those cases that have embraced it. Though uniform postratification practice can shed light upon the meaning of an ambiguous constitutional provision, the practice here is not uniform, and the core meaning of the constitutional guarantees is unambiguous.

___ U.S. at ___, 115 S.Ct. at ___, ___ L.Ed.2d at ___.

1. PROSECUTIONS TO WHICH THE RIGHT APPLIES

Page 1017. Add the following to note 1 after Duncan v. Louisiana:

The offense at issue in United States v. Nachtigal, ___ U.S. ___, 113 S.Ct. 1072, 122 L.Ed.2d 374 (1993) (per curiam) was driving under the influence and carried a maximum punishment of six months' imprisonment and a $5,000 fine. Alternatively, the court could impose probation not to exceed five years and to impose numerous conditions to the probation. Under *Blanton,* the Supreme Court held, this was a petty offense for which jury trial was not available. The maximum term of imprisonment—six months—creates a presumption that the offense is a petty one and the additional penalties "are not sufficiently severe to overcome this presumption." The fine could be $4,000 greater than was permissible in *Blanton,* but that was not controlling. Nor was the probation alternative:

> Like a monetary penalty, the liberty infringement caused by a term of probation is far less intrusive than incarceration. The discretionary probation conditions do not alter this conclusion; while they obviously entail a greater infringement on liberty than probation without attendant conditions, they do not approximate the severe loss of liberty caused by imprisonment for more than six months.

___ U.S. at ___, 113 S.Ct. at 1074, 122 L.Ed.2d at 380.

2. COMPOSITION OF THE JURY

Page 1034. Add the following before Note 2:

1a. A question not addressed in *Holland*—whether the Equal Protection Clause prohibits the prosecution from using peremptory challenges to exclude racial groups without regard to the race of the defendant—was answered in Powers v. Ohio, 499 U.S. 400, 111 S.Ct. 1364, 113 L.Ed.2d 411 (1991). Powers, a white male, was tried on two counts of murder and one of attempted murder. During jury selection, the prosecution used 7 of 10 peremptory challenges to remove Blacks from the jury panel. The trial court refused to require the prosecutor to justify those actions. The Ohio appellate courts rejected Powers' contention that this ruling violated the Equal Protection Clause, and affirmed the convictions. The United States Supreme Court, in an opinion by Justice Kennedy, reversed. Unlike in Holland v. Illinois, in this case the contention was an Equal Protection one, not a Sixth Amendment one. Justice Kennedy focused upon the interest of the system in assuring that all citizens have an equal opportunity to serve on juries:

> Jury service preserves the democratic element of the law, as it guards the rights of the parties and insures continued acceptance of the laws by all

> of the people * * *. It "affords ordinary citizens a valuable opportunity to participate in a process of government, an experience fostering, one hopes, a respect for law." [quoting from Duncan v. Louisiana, Casebook p. 1011] Indeed, with the exception of voting, for most citizens the honor and privilege of jury duty is their most significant opportunity to participate in the democratic process.

499 U.S. at 407, 111 S.Ct. at 1369, 113 L.Ed.2d at 423. The defendant is injured by exclusion of racial groups even if he is not a member of those groups:

> The purpose of the jury system is to impress upon the criminal defendant and the community as a whole that a verdict of conviction or acquittal is given in accordance with the law by persons who are fair. The verdict will not be accepted or understood in these terms if the jury is chosen by unlawful means at the outset. Upon these considerations, we find that a criminal defendant suffers a real injury when the prosecutor excluded jurors at his or her own trial on account of race.

499 U.S. at 413, 111 S.Ct. at 1372, 113 L.Ed.2d at 426. Justice Kennedy finally commented on the significance in *Batson* that the defendant was of the same race as the excluded members of the jury panel:

> Racial identity between the defendant and the excused person might in some cases be the explanation for the prosecution's adoption of the forbidden stereotype, and if the alleged race bias takes this form, it may provide one of the easier cases to establish both a prima facie case and a conclusive showing that wrongful discrimination has occurred. But to say that the race of the defendant may be relevant to discerning bias in some cases does not mean that it will be a factor in others, for race prejudice stems from various causes and may manifest itself in different forms.

499 U.S. at 416, 111 S.Ct. at 1373–74, 113 L.Ed.2d at 429. Justice Scalia, the author of the opinion for the Court in Holland v. Illinois, dissented in an opinion joined in by Chief Justice Rehnquist.

1b. Does *Batson* apply to civil suits between private parties? Petitioner in Edmonson v. Leesville Concrete Co., Inc., 500 U.S. 614, 111 S.Ct. 2077, 114 L.Ed.2d 660 (1991), a black construction worker, sued for injuries suffered on the work site. During jury selection, Leesville used 2 of its 3 peremptory challenges to remove blacks from the panel. The jury consisted of 11 whites and one black. The District Court rejected petitioner's *Batson* claim on the ground that decision applied only in criminal cases. The Supreme Court, in an opinion by Justice Kennedy, held that under Powers v. Ohio race-based use of strikes violates the excluded persons' equal protection rights. Although Leesville is a private party, its use of strikes was state action because strikes are authorized by law and can be used only in a court proceeding. The case was remanded for a determination whether petitioner had made a prima facie case of racial discrimination in the defendant's use of strikes. Justice O'Connor, joined by Chief Justice Rehnquist and Justice Scalia, dissented on the ground that the defendant's use of strikes did not constitute state action. Justice Scalia dissented separately, with the observation that the decision

> will not necessarily be a net help rather than hindrance to minority litigants in obtaining racially diverse juries. In criminal cases, *Batson v. Kentucky* * * * already prevents the *prosecution* from using race-based strikes. The

> effect of today's decision (which logically must apply to criminal prosecutions) will be to prevent the *defendant* from doing so—so that the minority defendant can no longer seek to prevent an all-white jury, or to seat as many jurors of his own race as possible. To be sure, it is ordinarily more difficult to *prove* race-based strikes of white jurors, but defense counsel can generally be relied upon to do what we say the Constitution requires. So in criminal cases, today's decision represents a net loss to the minority litigant.

500 U.S. at 644, 111 S.Ct. at 2095, 114 L.Ed.2d at 689.

1c. Justice Scalia's prediction that *Batson* would be held to apply to peremptory challenges by criminal defendants materialized in Georgia v. McCollum, ___ U.S. ___, 112 S.Ct. 2348, 120 L.Ed.2d 33 (1992). The State filed a motion requesting an order from the trial court to preclude Respondent, who is white, from using strikes to eliminate African–Americans from his criminal jury in a trial in which the victims were African–American. The trial court denied this motion and the Georgia Supreme Court affirmed in an interlocutory appeal. The Supreme Court, in an opinion by Justice Blackmun, reversed and held that *Batson* applies to strikes used by criminal defendants:

> Be it at the hands of the State or the defense, if a court allows jurors to be excluded because of group bias, it is a willing participant in a scheme that could only undermine the very foundation of our system of justice—our citizens' confidence in it. Just as public confidence in criminal justice is undermined by a conviction in a trial where racial discrimination has occurred in jury selection, so is public confidence undermined where a defendant, assisted by racially discriminatory peremptory strikes, obtains an acquittal.

___ U.S. at ___, 112 S.Ct. at 2354, 120 L.Ed.2d at 45. The Court then sought to distinguish cases in which criminal defendants have been held to have a constitutional right to question potential jurors about racial attitudes:

> [A] defendant has the right to an impartial jury that can view him without racial animus, which so long has distorted our system of criminal justice. We have, accordingly, held that there should be a mechanism for removing those on the venire whom the defendant has specific reason to believe would be incapable of confronting and suppressing their racism. See Ham v. South Carolina, 409 U.S. 524, 526–527 (1973) * * *.
>
> But there is a distinction between exercising a peremptory challenge to discriminate invidiously against jurors on account of race and exercising a peremptory challenge to remove an individual juror who harbors racial prejudice. This Court firmly has rejected the view that assumptions of partiality based on race provide a legitimate basis for disqualifying a person as an impartial juror.

___ U.S. at ___, 112 S.Ct. at 2358–59, 120 L.Ed.2d at 51. Justice Thomas concurred in the judgment with the comment, "I am certain that black criminal defendants will rue the day that this court ventured down this road that inexorably will lead to the elimination of peremptory strikes." Justice O'Connor dissented on the ground that there is no state action when a criminal defendant exercises a peremptory challenge.

1d. Does Batson apply to strikes based on gender? Petitioner in J.E.B. v. Alabama ex rel. T.B., ___ U.S. ___, 114 S.Ct. 1419, 128 L.Ed.2d 89 (1994) was the respondent in a paternity suit. The State used 9 of its 10 strikes to remove men from the jury panel, while Petitioner used 9 of his 10 strikes to remove women from the panel. The jury was composed entirely of women. Petitioner was adjudicated the father of the child and ordered to pay support. Before the Supreme Court, he claimed that the State's use of its strikes violated equal protection of the laws. The Court, in an opinion by Justice Blackmun, held that the State's use of strikes to remove men from the jury panel violated equal protection of the laws:

> Discrimination in jury selection, whether based on race or on gender, causes harm to the litigants, the community, and the individual jurors who are wrongfully excluded from participation in the judicial process. The litigants are harmed by the risk that the prejudice which motivated the discriminatory selection of the jury will infect the entire proceedings * * *. The community is harmed by the State's participation in the perpetuation of invidious group stereotypes and the inevitable loss of confidence in our judicial system that state-sanctioned discrimination in the courtroom engenders.

___ U.S. at ___, 114 S.Ct. at 1427, 128 L.Ed.2d at 104. Justice O'Connor, concurring, would limit the equal protection principle to actions by the government. Justice Scalia, joined by The Chief Justice and Justice Thomas, dissented.

Page 1038. Add the following after Note 7:

8. In Hernandez v. New York, 500 U.S. 352, 111 S.Ct. 1859, 114 L.Ed.2d 395 (1991), the Court addressed the question what showing must be made to justify the use of peremptory challenges on racial groups. Hernandez, identified in the Supreme Court's opinion as a "Latino," was on trial for attempted murder. The prosecutor used four peremptory challenges to exclude Latino potential jurors. A *Batson* claim was made with respect to two of those panel members. The prosecutor, without waiting for the trial court to rule on whether a *prima facie* showing had been made, volunteered that the reason he struck those two was that he was not persuaded they would be able to accept the official interpretation of Spanish language testimony because they were bilingual. This was based on their responses to that question on *voir dire* and their demeanor while responding. He added that since the defendant, victims, and all the civilian witnesses were Latino, he had no reason to exclude Latinos from the jury. The trial court found no *Batson* violation, which was upheld by the New York appellate courts on direct appeal from Hernandez' conviction. The United States Supreme Court, in a plurality opinion authored by Justice Kennedy and joined in by The Chief Justice and Justices White and Souter, affirmed. Because the prosecutor volunteered an explanation for his strikes, the question whether defendant had made a prima facie case of discrimination became moot. The prosecutor's neutral explanation—one based on something other than the race of the juror—was that

> the challenges rested neither on the intention to exclude Latino or bilingual jurors, nor on stereotypical assumptions about Latinos or bilinguals. The prosecutor's articulated basis for these challenges divided potential jurors into two classes: those whose conduct during *voir dire* would persuade him they might have difficulty in accepting the translator's rendition of Spanish-language testimony and those potential jurors who gave no such reason for doubt. Each category would include both Latinos and non-Latinos. While

> the prosecutor's criterion might well result in the disproportionate removal of prospective Latino jurors, that disproportionate impact does not turn the prosecutor's actions into a *per se* violation of the Equal Protection Clause.

500 U.S. at 361, 111 S.Ct. at 1867, 114 L.Ed.2d at 407. Once the prosecutor offered race-neutral explanations, the trial court was required to find whether the defendant had established purposeful discrimination. An appellate court can set aside such a finding only if it is clearly erroneous. Justice O'Connor, joined by Justice Scalia, concurred in the judgment, commenting,

> if, as in this case, the trial court believes the prosecutor's nonracial justification, and that finding is not clearly erroneous, that is the end of the matter. *Batson* does not require that a prosecutor justify a jury strike at the level of a for-cause challenge. It also does not require that the justification be unrelated to race. *Batson* requires only that the prosecutor's reason for striking a juror not *be* the juror's race.

500 U.S. at 375, 111 S.Ct. at 1875, 114 L.Ed.2d at 416. Justice Stevens, joined by Justice Marshall and in part by Justice Blackmun, dissented.

9. The Court refined somewhat the procedural steps in the trial litigation of a *Batson* claim in its *per curiam* opinion in Purkett v. Elem, ___ U.S. ___, 115 S.Ct. 1769, 131 L.Ed.2d 834 (1995). After the prosecutor struck two African-American panelists, respondent made a *Batson* objection. The prosecutor explained the strike of one panelist because he had long unkempt hair, a mustache and a goatee type beard. He explained striking the second panelist because he also had a mustache and goatee type beard. He added that those were the only members of the panel with facial hair. Further, the second panelist had once been the victim of a robbery with a sawed-off shotgun and the prosecutor expressed concern that he would not therefore regard the unarmed robbery being tried as robbery. The trial court overruled the *Batson* objection. On federal habeas following conviction, the Eighth Circuit found the trial court had not complied with *Batson* because the prosecutor's statement did not explain how the objectionable features would affect each person's ability to perform duties as a juror in the case.

The Supreme Court reversed. *Batson* claims require a three step procedure in the trial court: (1) a prima facie case of discrimination by the claimant, (2) a neutral explanation for the strike in question by the party exercising the challenged strike, and (3) a showing of purposeful discrimination by the claimant. The Court of Appeals erroneously combined steps (2) and (3). Step (2) merely requires that the explanation be non-discriminatory. It does not require that the explanation must relate to trial strategy. Once a non-discriminatory explanation is provided, then the burden shifts to the *Batson* claimant to show purposeful discrimination. So long as the step (2) explanation is race-neutral, it doesn't matter that it is "silly or superstitious." Such an explanation may fail, but only at step (3) and only as part of the conclusion that the claimant has shown purposeful discrimination.

Justice Stevens, joined by Justice Breyer, dissented.

3. THE JURY SIZE AND AGREEMENT REQUIRED

Page 1047. Add the following after Note 4:

5. Must the jury agree on a single legal theory of an offense when more than one have been charged and submitted to it? In Schad v. Arizona, 501 U.S.

624, 111 S.Ct. 2491, 115 L.Ed.2d 555 (1991), petitioner was charged with first-degree murder by premeditated killing and by killing in perpetration of robbery. There was evidence in support of each theory. The jury was instructed to return a verdict of not guilty, guilty of first-degree murder, or guilty of the lesser included offense of second degree murder, but was not required to agree upon which theory of first degree murder it found proved. The jury returned a verdict of guilty of first degree murder and the death sentence was imposed. Petitioner's contention that this procedure violated the Due Process Clause was rejected by the Court. In a plurality opinion by Justice Souter, joined by The Chief Justice and Justices O'Connor and Kennedy, the issue was characterized as whether under Arizona law first-degree murder is a single crime or whether premeditated murder and felony murder are separate crimes. Acknowledging that "nothing in our history suggests that the Due Process Clause would permit a State to convict anyone under a charge of 'Crime' so generic that any combination of jury findings of embezzlement, reckless driving, murder, burglary, tax evasion, or littering, for example, would suffice for conviction," this is not such a case. The Arizona court has determined that there is only one offense of first-degree murder and the Supreme Court is not free to take a different view of Arizona law; the only question is whether the view taken by the Arizona court is constitutional. Both premeditated killing and felony-murder are simply different forms of *mens rea.* Historically, each has simply been a different way of defining the same criminal offense. Finally, felony murder can be regarded as the moral equivalent of premeditated killing. Justice Scalia, concurring, placed emphasis upon the historical roots of the Arizona practice:

> Submitting killing in the course of a robbery and premeditated killing to the jury under a single charge is not some novel composite that can be subjected to the indignity of "fundamental fairness" review. It was the norm when this country was founded, was the norm when the Fourteenth Amendment was adopted in 1868, and remains the norm today. Unless we are here to invent a Constitution rather than enforce one, it is impossible that a practice as old as the common law and still in existence in the vast majority of States does not provide that process which is "due."

501 U.S. at ___, 111 S.Ct. at 2507, 115 L.Ed.2d at 577–78. Justice White, joined by Justices Marshall, Blackmun and Stevens, dissenting, took issue with the plurality's characterization of the two legal theories as simply alternative *mens rea* for the offense of first degree murder:

> [I]t is entirely possible that half of the jury believed the defendant was guilty of premeditated murder and not guilty of felony murder/robbery, while half believed exactly the reverse. [T]he plurality affirms this conviction without knowing that even a single element of either of the ways for proving first-degree murder, except the fact of a killing, has been found by a majority of the jury, let alone found unanimously by the jury as required by Arizona law. A defendant charged with first-degree murder is at least entitled to a verdict—something petitioner did not get in this case as long as the possibility exists that no more than six jurors voted for any one element of first-degree murder, except the fact of a killing.

501 U.S. at ___, 111 S.Ct. at 2509, 115 L.Ed.2d at 580.

6. What should happen when theories are presented to a jury in the alternative, a general verdict of guilty is returned, and the evidence is insuffi-

cient to support one of those theories? Petitioner in Griffin v. United States, ___ U.S. ___, 112 S.Ct. 466, 116 L.Ed.2d 371 (1991) was charged with conspiracy to defraud the United States Government. Two objects of the conspiracy were charged: defrauding the Internal Revenue Service and defrauding the Drug Enforcement Administration. The jury was instructed to return a verdict of guilty if it found that petitioner participated in either of the two objects of the conspiracy. The jury returned a general verdict of guilty. The Government conceded there was insufficient evidence that petitioner conspired to defraud the DEA. The Supreme Court, in an opinion by Justice Scalia, held that the verdict could stand despite the insufficiency of evidence.

The Court distinguished prior cases in which the theories submitted were based upon constitutionally protected conduct or in which the theories were not authorized by law. Evidence insufficiency is different:

> Jurors are not generally equipped to determine whether a particular theory of conviction submitted to them is contrary to law—whether, for example, the action in question is protected by the Constitution, is time barred, or fails to come within the statutory definition of the crime. When, therefore, jurors have been left the option of relying upon a legally inadequate theory, there is no reason to think that their own intelligence and expertise will save them from that error. Quite the opposite is true, however, when they have been left the option of relying upon a factually inadequate theory, since jurors *are* well equipped to analyze the evidence * * *.

___ U.S. at ___, 112 S.Ct. at 474, 116 L.Ed.2d at 382–83. Justice Blackmun concurred in the judgment; Justice Thomas did not participate.

C. CONFRONTATION, CROSS-EXAMINATION AND COMPULSORY PROCESS TO OBTAIN WITNESSES

1. CONFRONTATION

Page 1070. Add the following after Note 7:

7a. The Petitioner in White v. Illinois, ___ U.S. ___, 112 S.Ct. 736, 116 L.Ed.2d 848 (1992) was seen exiting the bedroom of a four-year old girl by her babysitter who was awakened by the girl's screams. The babysitter recognized the petitioner as a friend of the girl's mother. The girl told the babysitter that petitioner had engaged in sexual contact with her. About 30 minutes later, she told her mother the same story and about 45 minutes after the alleged assault, she told the same story to a police officer. About 4 hours after the alleged assault she told the same story first to a nurse and then to a doctor at a local hospital.

Statements by the babysitter, mother, police officer, nurse and doctor were admitted into evidence over hearsay and confrontation objections. The girl was called as a witness but did not testify. Petitioner was convicted of various offenses. The Supreme Court, in an opinion by The Chief Justice, affirmed the convictions.

The Court rejected as coming too late in history the *amicus curiae* arguments of the United States Government that the Confrontation Clause should be restricted to efforts to prove criminal charges by ex parte affidavits, that is, "where the circumstances surrounding the out-of-court statement's utterance suggest that the statement has been made for the principal purpose of accusing or incriminating the defendant." In this case, the girl's statements to her babysitter, mother and the police officer came within the traditional exception to the hearsay rule for spontaneous declarations while the last two statements came within the traditional exception for statements made in the course of receiving medical treatment:

> A statement that has been offered in a moment of excitement—without the opportunity to reflect on the consequences of one's exclamation—may justifiably carry more weight with a trier of fact than a similar statement offered in the relative calm of the courtroom. Similarly, a statement made in the course of procuring medical services, where the declarant knows that a false statement may cause misdiagnosis or mistreatment, carries special guarantees of credibility that a trier of fact may not think replicated by courtroom testimony.

___ U.S. at ___, 112 S.Ct. at 742–43, 116 L.Ed.2d at 859. The Court concluded that "where proffered hearsay has sufficient guarantees of reliability to come within a firmly rooted exception to the hearsay rule, the Confrontation Clause is satisfied."

Contrary to petitioner's contention, Coy v. Iowa and Maryland v. Craig do not require any showing of necessity for the statements at issue to be admitted in this case. Those cases "involved only the question of what *in-court* procedures are constitutionally required to guarantee a defendant's confrontation right once a witness is testifying. Such a question is quite separate from that of what requirements the Confrontation Clause imposes as a predicate for the introduction of out-of-court declarations."

Justice Thomas, joined by Justice Scalia, concurred in the judgment. He would hold that the

> Confrontation Clause is implicated by extrajudicial statements only insofar as they are contained in formalized testimonial materials, such as affidavits, depositions, prior testimony, or confessions. It was this discrete category of testimonial materials that was historically abused by prosecutors as a means to depriving criminal defendants of the benefit of the adversary process . . . and under this approach, the Confrontation Clause would not be construed to extend beyond the historical evil to which it was directed.

___ U.S. at ___, 112 S.Ct. at 747, 116 L.Ed.2d at 865.

Page 1072. Add the following to Note 8 after Maryland v. Craig before the last paragraph beginning on this page:

Whether a federal criminal trial can begin under Rule 43 if the accused does not appear was presented in Crosby v. United States, ___ U.S. ___, 113 S.Ct. 748, 122 L.Ed.2d 25 (1993). Crosby failed to appear for trial, although his attorney and three codefendants were present. After several days of searching failed to turn him up, the district judge began trial without him. He was convicted. Six months later he was apprehended in another state and brought back to the trial court for sentencing. Under Rule 43, the Supreme Court ruled, the trial court erred in beginning Crosby's trial without him present. "The language, history, and logic of Rule 43," it reasoned, "support a straightforward interpretation that prohibits the trial *in absentia* of a defendant who is not present at the beginning of trial." In explanation, Justice Blackmun offered for the Court:

> [W]e do not find the distinction between pre- and midtrial flight so far-fetched as to convince us that Rule 43 cannot mean what it says. As a general matter, the costs of suspending a proceeding already under way will be greater than the cost of postponing a trial not yet begun. If a clear line is to be drawn marking the point at which the costs of delay are likely to outweigh the interests of the defendant and society in having the defendant present, the commencement of trial is at least a plausible place at which to draw that line.
>
> There are additional practical reasons for distinguishing between flight before and flight during a trial. * * * [T]he Rule treats midtrial flight as a knowing and voluntary waiver of the right to be present. Whether or not the right constitutionally may be waived in other circumstances—and we express no opinion here on that subject—the defendant's initial presence serves to assure that any waiver is indeed knowing. "Since the notion that trial may be commenced in absentia still seems to shock most lawyers, it would hardly seem appropriate to impute knowledge that this will occur to their clients." Starkey, Trial in Absentia, 54 N.Y.St.B.J. 30, 34, n. 28 (1982). It is unlikely, on the other hand, " 'that a defendant who flees from a courtroom in the midst of a trial—where judge, jury, witnesses and lawyers are present and ready to continue—would not know that as a consequence the trial could continue in his absence.' " Taylor v. United States, 414 U.S. 17, 20, 94 S.Ct. 194, 196, 38 L.Ed.2d 174 (1973), quoting from Chief Judge Coffin's opinion, 478 F.2d 689, 691 (CA1 1973), for the Court of Appeals in that case. Moreover, a rule that allows an ongoing trial to continue when a defendant disappears deprives the defendant of the option of gambling on an acquittal knowing that he can terminate the trial if it seems that the verdict will go against him—an option that might otherwise appear preferable to the costly, perhaps unnecessary, path of becoming a fugitive from the outset.

___ U.S. at ___, 113 S.Ct. at 752–53, 122 L.Ed.2d at 32. Having thus resolved the case, the Court emphasized that it was not reaching Crosby's claim that his trial *in absentia* was prohibited by the United States Constitution. ___ U.S. at ___, 113 S.Ct. at 753, 122 L.Ed.2d at 33.

Chapter 24

EFFECTIVE ASSISTANCE OF COUNSEL

A. THE RIGHT TO HAVE COUNSEL BE "EFFECTIVE"

Page 1121. Add the following new note after Strickland v. Washington:

1b. *Strickland's* test was developed—perhaps only for very unusual situations—in Lockhart v. Fretwell, ___ U.S. ___, 113 S.Ct. 838, 122 L.Ed.2d 180 (1993). In 1985, upon proof that he killed the victim in the course of a robbery, Fretwell was convicted of capital felony murder in an Arkansas court. At the penalty stage, the State sought the death penalty and argued that the facts showed two aggravating circumstances: (a) that the murder was committed for pecuniary gain; and (b) that the murder was committed to facilitate Fretwell's escape. Shortly before the trial, the Eighth Circuit Court of Appeals had held in Collins v. Lockhart, 754 F.2d 258 (8th Cir.), cert. denied, 474 U.S. 1013, 106 S.Ct. 546, 88 L.Ed.2d 475 (1985) that a death sentence in a felony murder case was unconstitutional if it was based upon an aggravating factor that duplicated an underlying element of the felony. Fretwell's lawyer did not object to the trial judge's submission to the jury of the first aggravating circumstance urged by the State, even though reliance upon it was almost certainly contrary to *Collins.* The jury found the first aggravating circumstance to have been proved and sentenced Fretwell to death.

In later federal habeas corpus proceedings, Fretwell argued that he had been denied the effective assistance of counsel because defense counsel had not raised *Collins* in connection with the sentencing proceeding. By this time, however, *Collins* had been overruled as inconsistent with an intervening decision of the Supreme Court. Thus Fretwell challenged his counsel's performance on the basis of counsel's failure to raise an argument that was "good law" at the time of trial but at the time of his attack was recognized as without ultimate legal merit. The lower federal courts granted Fretwell relief. Counsel's failure to invoke *Collins* constituted deficient performance under *Strickland.* If counsel had invoked *Collins,* the trial judge would not have permitted the State to rely upon their first proffered aggravating circumstance, the jury would not have found the other circumstance shown by the evidence, and the jury would not have sentenced Fretwell to death. Thus Fretwell had established prejudice under *Strickland.*

The Supreme Court reversed, concluding that the lower federal courts had erred in finding that Fretwell showed prejudice. Defendants are afforded the Sixth Amendment right to counsel, Chief Justice Rehnquist explained for the majority, to protect their right to a fair—that is, reliable—trial. *Strickland's* test reflects this concern with reliability.

> Thus, an analysis focusing solely on mere outcome determination, without attention to whether the result of the proceeding was fundamentally unfair or unreliable, is defective. To set aside a conviction or sentence solely

> because the outcome would have been different but for counsel's error may grant the defendant a windfall to which the law does not entitle him.
>
> * * *
>
> The result of the sentencing proceeding in the present case was neither unfair nor unreliable. * * *

___ U.S. at ___, 113 S.Ct. at 842–43, 122 L.Ed.2d at 189–90.

Under *Strickland,* the Court agreed, whether counsel performed acceptably is to be viewed as of the time of the conduct challenged. Whether a defendant was prejudiced, however, is not to be determined under such a "rule of contemporary assessment." If counsel's ineffectiveness does not deprive a defendant of any substantive or procedural right to which the law—as it is later or ultimately known to be—entitles the defendant, no unreliability or unfairness results and there has been no prejudice. Since Fretwell is now known not to have been entitled to have the trial judge follow *Collins,* he suffered no prejudice from counsel's deficiency in failing to argue *Collins.* ___ U.S. at ___, 113 S.Ct. at 844, 122 L.Ed.2d at 191.

Justice O'Connor concurred to suggest that the Court's holding will affect only the unusual situations where defendants attempt to demonstrate prejudice based on considerations "that, as a matter of law, ought not inform the inquiry." In the vast majority of cases, she added, the Court's decision will have no effect on the prejudice inquiry under *Strickland.* ___ U.S. at ___, 113 S.Ct. at 845, 122 L.Ed.2d at 192 (O'Connor, J., concurring).

Justice Stevens, joined by Justice Blackmun, dissented, arguing that ineffective assistance of counsel claims should be evaluated under the law as it stood at the time of trial:

> Hindsight has no place in a Sixth Amendment jurisprudence that focuses, quite rightly, on protecting the adversarial balance at trial. * * * [A]s it happened, counsel's failure to object came at a time when it signified a breakdown in the adversarial process. A *post hoc* vision of what would have been the case years later has no bearing on the force of this showing.

___ U.S. at ___, 113 S.Ct. at 849, 122 L.Ed.2d at 197 (Stevens, J., dissenting).

Chapter 25

SENTENCING

B. STRUCTURING THE SENTENCING SYSTEM

2. CONTROLLING SENTENCING DISCRETION BY APPELLATE REVIEW

---

a. Appellate Review of Sentencing Considerations

Page 1150. Add the following before Note 2:

1a. United States v. Dunnigan, ___ U.S. ___, 113 S.Ct. 1111, 122 L.Ed.2d 445 (1993) raised the question of increasing punishment under the Sentencing Guidelines because the trial judge believed the defendant committed perjury in her trial testimony. Five witnesses testified for the Government as to defendant's involvement in cocaine trafficking. Defendant testified on her own behalf and denied any involvement. Following conviction, the trial judge increased the punishment under § C1.1 of the Guidelines because he believed she committed perjury at trial. The Court of Appeals set aside the sentence, distinguishing United States v. Grayson (Casebook p. 1147) on the ground that Grayson was based on the greater need for rehabilitation demonstrated by a defendant's committing perjury, while the Sentencing Guidelines base enhancement on punishment considerations. Also, the Court of Appeals believed that Grayson did not support the rigid enhancement imposed by the Guidelines.

The Supreme Court, in an opinion by Justice Kennedy for a unanimous Court, reversed. Grayson did not state that rehabilitation is the only justification for increasing a sentence because the defendant committed perjury. There are other considerations:

> [A] defendant who commits a crime and then perjures herself in an unlawful attempt to avoid responsibility is more threatening to society and less deserving of leniency than a defendant who does not so defy the trial process. The perjuring defendant's willingness to frustrate judicial proceedings to avoid criminal liability suggests the need for incapacitation and retribution is heightened as compared with the defendant charged with the same crime who allows judicial proceedings to progress without resorting to perjury.

___ U.S. at ___, 113 S.Ct. at 1118, 122 L.Ed.2d at 455. Just because a defendant testifies in his own defense and is convicted does not mean his testimony was perjurious:

> [A]n accused may give inaccurate testimony due to confusion, mistake or faulty memory. In other instances, an accused may testify to matters such as lack of capacity, insanity, duress or self-defense. Her testimony may be truthful, but the jury may nonetheless find the testimony insufficient to

> excuse criminal liability or prove lack of intent. For these reasons, if a defendant objects to a sentence enhancement resulting from her trial testimony, a district court must review the evidence and make independent findings necessary to establish a willful impediment to or obstruction of justice, or an attempt to do the same * * *.

___ U.S. at ___, 113 S.Ct. at 1117, 122 L.Ed.2d at 454.

b. Appellate Review of the Sentences Imposed

Page 1164. Add the following at the beginning of Notes:

.5. The Supreme Court re-visited the Solem v. Helm issue in Harmelin v. Michigan, 501 U.S. 957, 111 S.Ct. 2680, 115 L.Ed.2d 836 (1991). Petitioner was convicted of possessing 672 grams of cocaine and sentenced to a mandatory term of life imprisonment without possibility of parole. He contended the sentence violated Eighth Amendment because it was disproportionate to the crime and because it was mandatory. The Supreme Court upheld petitioner's sentence and in doing so delivered five different opinions. Justice Scalia announced the judgment of the Court and delivered an opinion. In Part V of that opinion, joined by Chief Justice Rehnquist and Justices O'Connor, Kennedy and Souter, the Court rejects the argument that the sentence in this case was cruel and unusual because it was mandatory and, therefore, precluded the sentencer from taking mitigating circumstances into account. "Severe, mandatory penalties may be cruel, but they are not unusual in the constitutional sense, having been employed in various forms throughout our Nation's history." It is true that a requirement of individualization of sentence has been imposed in death penalty cases but there is a "qualitative difference between death and all other penalties."

> It is true that petitioner's sentence is unique in that it is the second most severe known to the law; but life imprisonment *with* possibility of parole is also unique in that it is the third most severe. And if petitioner's sentence forecloses some "flexible techniques" for later reducing his sentence, * * * it does not foreclose all of them, since there remain the possibilities of retroactive legislative reduction and executive clemency. In some cases, moreover, there will be negligible difference between life without parole and other sentences of imprisonment—for example, a life sentence with eligibility for parole after 20 years, or even a lengthy term sentence without eligibility, given to a 65–year–old man. But even where the difference is the greatest, it cannot be compared with death.

501 U.S. at ___, 111 S.Ct. at 2702, 115 L.Ed.2d at 865. Justice Scalia, writing for himself and Chief Justice Rehnquist, contended that the Eighth Amendment does not prescribe a constitutional requirement of proportionality of penalty to offense and argued that *Solem* should be overruled. Justice Kennedy, joined by Justices O'Connor and Souter, rejected Justice Scalia's view of the Eighth Amendment and contended that "*stare decisis* counsels our adherence to the narrow proportionality principle that has existed in our Eighth Amendment jurisprudence for 80 years." He then compared the seriousness of petitioner's offense with that of Solem. The cocaine possessed in this case would produce between 32,500 and 65,000 doses. Petitioner's "crime threatened to cause grave harm to society:"

> Studies * * * demonstrate a direct nexus between illegal drugs and crimes of violence * * *. 57 percent of a national sample of males arrested in 1989 for homicide tested positive for illegal drugs * * *. The comparable statistics for assault, robbery, and weapons arrests were 55, 73 and 63 percent, respectively * * *. In Detroit, Michigan in 1988, 68 percent of a sample of male arrestees and 81 percent of a sample of female arrestees tested positive for illegal drugs * * *. And last year an estimated 60 percent of the homicides in Detroit were drug-related, primarily cocaine-related.

501 U.S. at ___, 111 S.Ct. at 2706, 115 L.Ed.2d at 870. Since petitioner's punishment is not disproportionate to his offense, there is no need to perform an analysis comparing his sentence to those imposed on others. As to the mandatory feature of the Michigan sentencing scheme,

> The scheme provides clear notice of the severe consequences that attach to possession of drugs in wholesale amounts, thereby giving force to one of the first purposes of criminal law—deterrence. In this sense, the Michigan scheme may be as fair, if not more so, than other sentencing systems in which the sentencer's discretion or the complexity of the scheme obscures the possible sanction for a crime, resulting in a shock to the offender who learns the severity of his sentence only after he commits the crime.

501 U.S. at ___, 111 S.Ct. at 2708, 115 L.Ed.2d at 873.

Justice White, joined by Justices Blackmun and Stevens, dissented, emphasizing the fact that this was petitioner's first criminal conviction. Examining the case in light of the factors in *Solem,* he would have found the sentence to violate the Eighth Amendment. Justice Marshall agreed with Justice White's opinion, except that portion asserting that the Eighth Amendment does not proscribe the death penalty. Justice Stevens, joined by Justice Blackmun, also agreed with Justice White's opinion but added that life without parole cannot purport to serve a rehabilitative purpose and that "no jurisdiction except Michigan has concluded that the offense belongs in a category where reform and rehabilitation are considered totally unattainable."

3. REDUCING DISCRETION BY "DETERMINATE" SENTENCING

---

b. Federal Reform: The Sentencing Reform Act of 1984

Page 1181. Add the following after Note 4:

5. Federal law authorizes a District Court to impose a sentence below a statutory or guidelines minimum if the Government has filed a motion stating the defendant has provided substantial assistance in the investigation or prosecution of another person. The petitioner in Wade v. United States, 504 U.S. 181, 112 S.Ct. 1840, 118 L.Ed.2d 524 (1992) pleaded guilty to an offense that carried a 10 year minimum sentence. At sentencing he asked the District Court to impose a sentence less than 10 years on the ground he had provided substantial assistance. The District Court refused, taking the position it lacked that power without a motion from the Government. The United States Supreme Court, in an opinion for a unanimous Court by Justice Souter, upheld this decision. A District Court lacks power to impose a sentence lower than a statutory minimum

or the minimum provided by guidelines unless the Government has filed a substantial assistance motion or unless the defendant can show that its failure to do so was based upon an unconstitutional motive, such as race or religion. This is the same standard that governs judicial review of prosecutorial charging decisions. Wade made no claim of unconstitutional motive. Wade also did not claim that the Government's failure to file a substantial assistance motion was a breach of a plea agreement.

6. In addition to guidelines, the United States Sentencing Commission publishes policy statements and commentaries. What weight should courts give to those "lesser" declarations from the Commission? In Williams v. United States, 503 U.S. ___, 112 S.Ct. 1112, 117 L.Ed.2d 341 (1992), the petitioner was convicted of possession of a firearm by a convicted felon. The District Court imposed a longer sentence than normally authorized by the sentencing guidelines on the basis of the petitioner's arrest record. While such action was not specifically prohibited by guidelines, it was done contrary to a policy statement that records of arrests for unadjudicated offenses can not be taken into account in this manner. The Supreme Court, in an opinion by Justice O'Connor, held that "[w]here ... a policy statement prohibits a district court from taking a specified action, the statement is an authoritative guide to the meaning of the applicable guideline. An error in interpreting such a policy statement could lead to an incorrect determination that a departure was appropriate." 503 U.S. at ___, 112 S.Ct. at 1119, 117 L.Ed.2d at 353. The Court vacated sentence and remanded for a determination whether the sentence was a result of the "error in interpreting" the policy statement or of authorized considerations in the case. Justice White, joined by Justice Kennedy, dissented.

The weight to be given to Commission commentaries was considered by the Court in Stinson v. United States, 508 U.S. ___, 113 S.Ct. 1913, 123 L.Ed.2d 598 (1993). Petitioner was also convicted of possession of a firearm by a convicted felon. The District Court sentenced him as a career offender based on a finding that the offense of possession of a firearm by a convicted felon is a "crime of violence" justifying that upward departure. Later, the Commission promulgated a commentary to the guidelines stating explicitly that possession of a firearm by a convicted felon is not a crime of violence under the career offender guidelines. The Supreme Court, in a unanimous opinion by Justice Kennedy, held that guidelines should be given a weight akin to an administrative agency's interpretation of its own legislative rules. "[P]rovided an agency's interpretation of its own regulations does not violate the Constitution or a federal statute, it must be given 'controlling weight unless it is plainly erroneous or inconsistent with the regulation.'" 508 U.S. at ___, 113 S.Ct. at 1919, 123 L.Ed.2d at 608. The Court also addressed the relationship between amendments in the commentary, as occurred in this case, and prior inconsistent appellate court interpretations of the underlying guideline:

> Although amendments to guidelines provisions are one method of incorporating revisions, another method open to the Commission is amendment of the commentary, if the guideline which the commentary interprets will bear the construction. Amended commentary is binding on the federal courts even though it is not reviewed by Congress, and prior judicial constructions of a particular guideline cannot prevent the Commission from adopting a conflicting interpretation that satisfies the standard we set forth today.

508 U.S. at ___, 113 S.Ct. at 1919, 123 L.Ed.2d at 608–09. The Court remanded the case to the Court of Appeals for it to determine what effect, if any, the amended commentary should be given in petitioner's case.

Chapter 26

APPEAL AND COLLATERAL ATTACK

B. APPEAL

Page 1237. Add the following to the first paragraph:

However, the United States Supreme Court held in Brecht v. Abrahamson, 507 U.S. ___, 113 S.Ct. 1710, 123 L.Ed.2d 353 (1993) that when review is obtained in federal habeas corpus proceedings the proper harmless error standard is the less onerous one of Kotteakos v. United States, 328 U.S. 750, 66 S.Ct. 1239, 90 L.Ed. 1557 (1946)—whether the constitutional violation "had substantial and injurious effect or influence in determining the jury's verdict"—rather than the *Chapman* standard that is applied on direct appeal. See also, O'Neal v. McAninch, ___ U.S. ___, 115 S.Ct. 992, 994, 130 L.Ed.2d 947, 952 (1995) (under *Brecht,* federal judge in habeas proceeding who is in grave doubt whether a trial error in state proceeding had "substantial and injurious effect or influence in determining the jury's verdict" is to treat error as *not* harmless).

Page 1242. Add the following after Note 3:

3a. In a series of decisions, the Court has issued orders prospectively denying *in forma pauperis* status to pro se litigants who have repeatedly filed frivolous petitions in the United States Supreme Court. See In re McDonald, 489 U.S. 180, 109 S.Ct. 993, 103 L.Ed.2d 158 (1989) (73 filings with the Supreme Court since 1971); In re Sindram, 498 U.S. 177, 111 S.Ct. 596, 112 L.Ed.2d 599 (1991) (24 filings with Supreme Court during October 1990 Term); In re Demos, 500 U.S. 16, 111 S.Ct. 1569, 114 L.Ed.2d 20 (1991) (32 filings with the Supreme Court since 1988). These cases culminated in an order amending Rule 39 of the Rules of the Supreme Court of the United States to add Rule 39.8:

> If satisfied that a petition for a writ of certiorari, jurisdictional statement, or petition for an extraordinary writ, as the case may be, is frivolous or malicious, the Court may deny a motion for leave to proceed *in forma pauperis.*

In re Amendment to Rule 39, 500 U.S. 13, 111 S.Ct. 1572, 114 L.Ed.2d 15 (1991). Justice Stevens, joined by Justice Blackmun, dissented. Justice Marshall dissented with the comment,

> This Court once had a great tradition: "All men and women are entitled to their day in Court." That guarantee has now been conditioned on monetary worth. It now will read: "All men and women are entitled to their day in Court only if they have the *means* and the *money.*"

500 U.S. at 14, 111 S.Ct. at 1573–74, 114 L.Ed.2d at 18. A denial of *in forma pauperis* status has the effect of requiring the payment of a $300 filing fee and the costs of printing the documents filed.

In In re Anderson, ___ U.S. ___, 114 S.Ct. 1606, 128 L.Ed.2d 332 (1994), the Court, per curiam, invoked Rule 39.8 with respect to the filing of petitions for extraordinary writs. Since the abuse had been limited principally to extraordinary writs, the Court restricted the Rule 39.8 action to extraordinary writs. Justice Stevens, joined by Justice Blackmun, dissented.

3b. In some circumstances, a convicted defendant may lose an otherwise available right of appeal by escaping from custody. In Ortega–Rodriguez v. United States, ___ U.S. ___, 113 S.Ct. 1199, 122 L.Ed.2d 581 (1993), the Supreme Court recounted that it has since 1876 approved of federal courts dismissing appeals of defendants who are fugitives from justice during the pendency of their appeals and has upheld state provisions for dismissal of appeals under similar circumstances. Dismissal is justified in part because any judgments affirming the convictions would be unenforceable. Further, flight or escape can properly be viewed as tantamount to waiver or abandonment of the pending appeal. Dismissal discourages escapes. It also promotes efficient and dignified appellate processes. ___ U.S. at ___, 113 S.Ct. at 1203–05, 122 L.Ed.2d at 591–93.

Ortega–Rodriguez, however, had fled after conviction but before sentencing. He was sentenced *in absentia*. Nearly a year later, he was apprehended. The district court granted his motion for resentencing and sentenced him to a somewhat less severe sentence than that imposed while he was a fugitive. When he sought to appeal, the Government moved to dismiss the appeal because he had been a fugitive after his conviction; the Court of Appeals granted the motion. Reversing by a 5–to–4 vote, the Supreme Court held that a federal appellate court cannot dismiss an appeal because the defendant was a fugitive before the appellate process began, unless the appellate court concludes that the defendant's flight significantly interfered with the appellate process.

Such defendants pose no risk that appellate courts' judgments cannot be enforced, Justice Stevens explained for the majority. Nor do they generally interfere with the orderly and efficient operation of the appellate process or affront the dignity of the appellate court. District courts are better equipped to fashion appropriate penalties for escape of defendants while the cases are before those courts; thus dismissal of appeals is not sufficiently necessary to deter pre-appeal escapes. ___ U.S. at ___, 113 S.Ct. at 1205–08, 122 L.Ed.2d at 594–97. Dismissal of an appeal is appropriate, however, if on the facts of a particular case an appellate court finds that a defendant's pre-appeal escape actually and substantially interfered with the appellate process. This might occur, for example, if escape prevented the defendant's appeal from being joined with that of his codefendants for expeditious decision together. ___ U.S. at ___, 113 S.Ct. at 1209, 122 L.Ed.2d at 597–98.

Chief Justice Rehnquist, joined by three other justices, argued that dismissal in pre-appeal escape cases was justified as a general rule. Defendants who escape pose a threat to the orderly operation of the appellate process and flout the authority of the judicial process of which the appellate court is an integral part. Moreover, dismissals serve the important interest of discouraging escapes. ___ U.S. at ___, 113 S.Ct. at 1211–13, 122 L.Ed.2d at 599–603 (Rehnquist, C.J., dissenting).

Whether *Ortega–Rodriguez* portended federal constitutional limits on fugitive dismissal rules was raised in Goeke v. Branch, ___ U.S. ___, 115 S.Ct. 1275, 131 L.Ed.2d 152 (1995) (per curiam). Branch, a defendant in a Missouri prosecution, had escaped after conviction but before sentencing. She was quickly captured and sentenced. The state appellate court dismissed her attempted appeal based on Missouri's fugitive dismissal rule. Branch sought federal habeas corpus relief and the Eighth Circuit held she was entitled to it. Due process, it reasoned, bars a state from applying a fugitive dismissal rule in a case where the appellant's escape did not delay appellate proceedings, inconvenience the appellate court, or otherwise affect the appellate process. The United States Supreme Court reversed on the ground that any federal constitutional rule barring a state from enforcing its fugitive dismissal rule would be a new rule not enforceable in a federal habeas corpus proceeding. Rejecting Branch's argument that the rule applied by the Eighth Circuit was not a new rule, the Court found no basis for the intermediate court's position in existing or well-settled authority. In *Ortega–Rodriguez,* the Court acknowledged, it had stated "that absent some adverse effect of pre-appeal flight on the appellate process, 'the defendant's former fugitive status may well lack the kind of connection to the appellate process that would justify an appellate sanction of dismissal.'" Nevertheless, the Court explained in *Goeke,* the rationale for *Ortega–Rodriguez* was limited to the Court's supervisory powers and thus did not suggest that dismissal of a fugitive's appeal implicated constitutional principles.

> As we explained in Allen v. Georgia, [166 U.S. 138, 140, 17 S.Ct. 525, 526, 41 L.Ed. 949 (1897)], where the Court upheld against constitutional attack the dismissal of the petition of a fugitive whose appeal was pending, "if the Supreme Court of a State has acted in consonance with the constitutional laws of a State and its own procedures, it could only be in very exceptional circumstances that this court would feel justified in saying that there had been a failure of due legal process. We might ourselves have pursued a different course in this case, but that is not the test." The Eighth Circuit converted a rule for the administration of the federal courts into a constitutional one.

___ U.S. at ___, 115 S.Ct. at 1278, 131 L.Ed.2d at 159. The Court emphasized, however, that it was not reaching the merits of Branch's contention that due process prohibits dismissal of appeals for escapes that do not affect the appellate process.

C. COLLATERAL ATTACK

Page 1250. Add the following to Note 1:

How should the "in custody" requirement be employed when the petitioner has received consecutive prison sentences? The petitioner in Garlotte v. Fordice, ___ U.S. ___, 115 S.Ct. 1948, ___ L.Ed.2d ___ (1995) received a three year prison sentence on a marijuana charge and two life sentences of murder charges. The life sentences were imposed consecutively to the three year sentence. After serving the three year sentence, but while still incarcerated on the life sentences, petitioner filed a federal habeas petition challenging the validity of the three year sentence. The District Court denied the petition on the merits, but the Fifth Circuit dismissed the petition on the ground he was no longer in custody under the three year sentence. The Supreme Court, in an opinion by Justice Ginsburg, reversed. In Peyton v. Rowe, 391 U.S. 54, 88 S.Ct. 1549, 20 L.Ed.2d 426 (1968), the Court had held that a state prisoner is "in custody" with respect to a consecutive sentence that he had not yet started serving. This case is *Peyton* in reverse. The key feature in this case is that the three year sentence, although already served, continues to postpone petitioner's parole eligibility date on the two life sentences. Since successful challenge of that sentence would advance petitioner's parole eligibility date, he is still in custody under that sentence.

Page 1251. Add the following to Note 2 after 28 U.S.C.A. §§ 2254–2255:

In Withrow v. Williams, ___ U.S. ___, 113 S.Ct. 1745, 123 L.Ed.2d 407 (1993), by a 5–to–4 vote, the Court held that the *Stone* approach would not be applied when a state defendant sought federal habeas corpus on grounds that a confession obtained in violation of Miranda v. Arizona, 384 U.S. 436, 86 S.Ct. 1602, 16 L.Ed.2d 694 (1966) had been used to convict him. The reasons for not applying *Stone's* approach to *Miranda* claims, Justice Souter explained for the majority, rest in part upon differences between a state defendant's right under Mapp v. Ohio, 367 U.S. 643, 81 S.Ct. 1684, 6 L.Ed.2d 1081 (1961) to have evidence obtained in violation of the Fourth Amendment excluded from trial and *Miranda*. *Mapp* created no personal constitutional right; *Miranda's* requirements, in contrast, safeguard defendants' Fifth Amendment privilege against self-incrimination, "a fundamental *trial* right." *Mapp* protects privacy rights divorced from the correct ascertainment of guilt in criminal trials. *Miranda,* on the other hand "serves to guard against 'the use of unreliable statements at trial' " "[b]y bracing against 'the possibility of unreliable statements in every instance of in-custody interrogation[.]' "

Most importantly, Justice Souter continued, state prisoners barred from raising *Miranda* claims in federal habeas corpus would simply convert those claims into due process claims that involuntary confessions had been used. Federal courts' workload would not be lightened by limiting habeas petitioners' ability to raise *Miranda* claims; federal judges would simply be confronted with due process involuntariness rather than *Miranda* claims. Nor would this change in the form of claims made by state prisoners go far towards reducing tensions between the state and federal judicial systems. "[E]liminating review of *Miranda* claims," Justice Souter concluded, "would not significantly benefit the federal courts in their exercise of habeas jurisdiction, or advance the cause of federalism in any substantial way." ___ U.S. at ___, 113 S.Ct. at 1754, 123 L.Ed.2d at 420. The Chief Justice and Justices O'Connor, Scalia and Thomas dissented. Justice O'Connor explained that when a case is on collateral review, the "marginal" benefits of applying *Miranda* are outweighed by the costs of undercutting finality of state conviction, aggravating tension between state and federal courts, and sometimes requiring reversal of guilty persons' convictions when the passage of time makes reprosecutions impossible.

Page 1252. Add the following Note before Wainwright v. Sykes:

5. Is a claim that a person sentenced to death is innocent of the offense for which he was sentenced independently cognizable on federal habeas corpus? The petitioner in Herrera v. Collins, ___ U.S. ___, 113 S.Ct. 853, 122 L.Ed.2d 203 (1993) was convicted of the capital murder of a police officer and was sentenced to death. Later, he plead guilty to the related killing of another police officer. His conviction and sentence were upheld on direct appeal and on state and federal habeas. Under Texas law, motions for new trial based on newly discovered evidence can be made only within 30 days of sentencing. Ten years

after his conviction, petitioner urged in state habeas that he was actually innocent of the murders and produced three affidavits from relatives that his now-deceased brother committed the killings. The Supreme Court, in an opinion by The Chief Justice, held that a claim of actual innocence by a state prisoner is not cognizable on federal habeas corpus,

> [I]n state criminal proceedings the trial is the paramount event for determining the guilt or innocence of the defendant. Federal habeas review of state convictions has traditionally been limited to claims of constitutional violations occurring in the course of the underlying state criminal proceedings * * *. History shows that the traditional remedy for claims of innocence based on new evidence, discovered too late in the day to file a new trial motion, has been executive clemency.

___ U.S. at ___, 113 S.Ct. at 869, 122 L.Ed.2d at 203. The Court acknowledged "for the sake of argument in deciding this case" that "a truly persuasive demonstration of 'actual innocence' made after trial would render the execution of a defendant unconstitutional" but then asserted that the facts in *Herrera* fell far short of such a demonstration. Justice O'Connor, joined by Justice Kennedy, concurred while expressing doubt about the wisdom of the Court's dictum about a truly persuasive demonstration of actual innocence. She then examined all of the evidence in the case, including the affidavits attesting to petitioner's innocence, and concluded that it shows his guilt "overwhelmingly." Justice Scalia, joined by Justice Thomas, concurred with the observation that "[t]here is no basis * * * for finding in the Constitution a right to demand judicial consideration of newly discovered evidence of innocence brought forward after conviction." Justice White concurred on the explicit assumption that the position expressed in argument by the Court that relief would be granted on a persuasive showing of actual innocence would ultimately prevail. Justice Blackmun, joined in part by Justices Stevens and Souter, dissented and would have remanded the case to District Court to give petitioner an opportunity to prove his innocence.

Page 1258. Add the following after Note 3:

3a. The petitioner in Coleman v. Thompson, 501 U.S. 722, 111 S.Ct. 2546, 115 L.Ed.2d 640 (1991) was convicted in a Virginia state court of murder and given the death penalty. On direct appeal, the Virginia Supreme Court affirmed the conviction and sentence. Coleman then filed a petition for habeas corpus in the state trial court, alleging various additional federal constitutional grounds for relief. The state trial court conducted a two-day evidentiary hearing and denied all relief. Thirty-three days later, Coleman's attorney filed notice of appeal from that decision to the Virginia Supreme Court. On motion of the Commonwealth, that court dismissed the appeal because notice of appeal had not been given within 30 days of the habeas decision. Coleman then filed a petition for habeas corpus in the United States District Court, making the federal claims he had made in his direct appeal and state habeas proceedings. The District Court ruled that Coleman had procedurally defaulted the claims that had been made only in the state habeas proceeding by failing to file a timely notice of appeal; it also considered all the claims on the merits and denied them. This decision was affirmed by the United States Court of Appeals. The Supreme Court, in an opinion by Justice O'Connor, held that Coleman had procedurally defaulted those claims by filing notice of appeal 3 days late. Under the rule of Fay v. Noia [Casebook p. 1252], a procedural default cannot be found except upon a showing petitioner waived the state remedy by deliberately bypassing it and there was no contention the late notice of appeal was deliberate. However, the Court reasoned subsequent cases, primarily Wainwright v. Sykes [Casebook p. 1252], signal a change in emphasis from *Fay:*

> In all cases in which a state prisoner has defaulted his federal claims in state court pursuant to an independent and adequate state procedural rule, federal habeas review of the claims is barred unless the prisoner can demonstrate cause for the default and actual prejudice as a result of the alleged violation of federal law, or demonstrate that failure to consider the claims will result in a fundamental miscarriage of justice. *Fay* was based on a conception of federal/state relations that undervalued the importance of state procedural rules. The several cases after *Fay* that applied the cause and prejudice standard to a variety of state procedural defaults represent a different view. We now recognize the important interest in finality served by state procedural rules, and the significant harm to the States that results from the failure of federal courts to respect them.

501 U.S. at ___, 111 S.Ct. at 2565, 115 L.Ed.2d at 669. Coleman argued that his counsel was ineffective in filing notice of appeal late and that should be regarded as cause for excusing the procedural default. The Court rejected that argument,

> There is no constitutional right to an attorney in state post-conviction proceedings. Pennsylvania v. Finley, 481 U.S. 551, 107 S.Ct. 1990, 95 L.Ed.2d 539 (1987); Murray v. Giarratano, 492 U.S. 1, 109 S.Ct. 2765, 106 L.Ed.2d 1 (1989) * * *. Consequently, a petitioner cannot claim constitutionally ineffective assistance of counsel in such proceedings * * *. Coleman contends that it was his attorney's error that led to the late filing of his state habeas appeal. This error cannot be constitutionally ineffective, therefore Coleman must "bear the risk of attorney error that results in a procedural default."

501 U.S. at ___, 111 S.Ct. at 2566, 115 L.Ed.2d at 671. Justice Blackmun, joined by Justices Marshall and Stevens, dissented.

In a related opinion, Ylst v. Nunnemaker, 501 U.S. 797, 111 S.Ct. 2590, 115 L.Ed.2d 706 (1991), the Court dealt with the requirement of Harris v. Reed that a state procedural default requires an express statement of reliance on state law as applied to unexplained, memorandum decisions of state courts. Nunnemaker was convicted in a California state court of murder. The California Court of Appeals affirmed his conviction, rejecting a *Miranda* claim on the ground respondent had not raised it in the trial court. The California Supreme Court denied discretionary review. A state habeas petition was denied without opinion, as was a similar petition in the Court of Appeals. Finally, an original state habeas petition was denied by the California Supreme Court by memorandum decision that cited two cases not here relevant. Respondent filed a federal habeas petition alleging the *Miranda* violation, which was rejected by the United States District Court on the ground of state procedural default. The United States Court of Appeals reversed this decision under Harris v. Reed on the ground that since the California Supreme Court decision was not explicitly based on state grounds, it could not be said the decision was not based on federal grounds rather than state procedural requirements. The United States Supreme Court, in an opinion by Justice Scalia, reversed:

> The * * * question presented by the present case * * * is how federal courts in habeas proceedings are to determine whether an unexplained order (by which we mean an order whose text or accompanying opinion does not disclose the reason for the judgment) rests primarily on federal law. The question is not an easy one * * *.
>
> The problem we face arises * * * because many formulary orders are not meant to convey *anything* as to the reason for the decision. Attributing a reason is therefore both difficult and artificial. We think that the attribution necessary for federal habeas purposes can be facilitated, and sound results more often assured, by applying the following presumption: where there has been one reasoned state judgment rejecting a federal claim, later unexplained orders upholding that judgment or rejecting the same claim rest upon the same ground. If an earlier opinion "fairly appear[s] to rest primarily upon federal law," * * * we will presume that no procedural default has been invoked by a subsequent unexplained order that leaves the judgment or its consequences in place. Similarly where, as here, the last reasoned opinion on the claim explicitly imposes a procedural default, we will presume that a later decision rejecting the claim did not silently disregard that bar and consider the merits.

501 U.S. at ___, 111 S.Ct. at 2594, 115 L.Ed.2d at 716–17. While the presumption is rebuttable, it is not rebutted here. Therefore, the memorandum decision of the California Supreme Court did not alter the procedural default ruling of the earlier California Court of Appeals decision and federal habeas relief is barred under Coleman v. Thompson unless respondent can on remand establish cause and prejudice. Justice Blackmun, joined by Justices Marshall and Stevens, dissented.

Page 1260. Add the following to Notes:

6. The subject of abuse of the writ of habeas corpus was addressed in McCleskey v. Zant, 499 U.S. 467, 111 S.Ct. 1454, 113 L.Ed.2d 517 (1991). McCleskey was convicted of murder in a Georgia state court and given the death penalty. After losing appeals, he filed a state habeas corpus petition in which, among other grounds of relief, he claimed a custodial statement had been obtained in violation of Massiah v. United States [Casebook p. 555]. Relief was denied. He filed his first federal habeas petition, in which he made several claims, but not the Massiah claim. Relief was ultimately denied, as was relief on a second state habeas petition. McCleskey then filed his second federal habeas petition, alleging seven grounds of relief, including the Massiah claim missing from the first federal habeas petition. The United States District Court granted relief based on the Massiah claim. It also rejected an argument by the State that McCleskey had abused the federal writ by finding that he had not deliberately abandoned his Massiah claim by failing to raise it in the first federal petition. The United States Court of Appeals reversed the District Court, finding that McCleskey had deliberately abandoned the Massiah claim.

The United States Supreme Court, in an opinion by Justice Kennedy, affirmed the Court of Appeals. It held that a showing of deliberate abandonment was not required for abuse of the writ, that "the same standard [Wainwright v. Sykes] used to determine whether to excuse state procedural defaults should govern the determination of inexcusable neglect in the abuse of the writ context." 499 U.S. at 490, 111 S.Ct. at 1468, 113 L.Ed.2d at 542. The Court then attempted to define a process for resolving questions of writ abuse under this standard:

> When a prisoner files a second or subsequent application, the government bears the burden of pleading abuse of the writ. The government satisfies this burden if, with clarity and particularity, it notes petitioner's prior writ history, identifies the claims that appear for the first time, and alleges that petitioner has abused the writ. The burden to disprove abuse then becomes petitioner's. To excuse his failure to raise the claim earlier, he must show cause for failing to raise it and prejudice therefrom as those concepts have been defined in our procedural default decisions. The petitioner's opportunity to meet the burden of cause and prejudice will not include an evidentiary hearing if the district court determines as a matter of law that petitioner cannot satisfy the standard. If petitioner cannot show cause, the failure to raise the claim in an earlier petition may nonetheless be excused if he or she can show that a fundamental miscarriage of justice would result from a failure to entertain the claim.

499 U.S. at 494–95, 111 S.Ct. at 1470, 113 L.Ed.2d at 545. Finally, the Court concluded that "the requirement of cause * * * is based on the principle that petitioner must conduct a reasonable and diligent investigation aimed at including all relevant claims and grounds for relief in the first federal habeas petition." 499 U.S. at 498, 111 S.Ct. at 1472, 113 L.Ed.2d at 547. Justice Marshall, joined by Justices Blackmun and Stevens, dissented.

†